Discover!
Social Studies

5

Discover! Social Studies 5A

Published in Catasauqua, Pennsylvania by Discover Press, a division of Edovate Learning Corp.

334 2nd Street

Catasauqua, PA 18032

edovate.com

ISBN: 978-1-956330-14-4

Printed in United States of America

1st Edition

Chapter 1

Chapter 2

Chapter 3

Chapter 4

GRADE 5
Social Studies

Chapter 5

Chapter 6

Chapter 7

Lesson Objectives

By the end of this lesson, your student will be able to:

- define geography as the study of places and the relationship between people and their environments
- identify that geographers study physical geography and cultural geography
- examine different maps of Africa and determine which show physical geography and which show cultural geography
- determine a story that a map can tell about an area based on its features

Supporting Your Student

Explore

Your student may benefit from hearing your observations about the map to help generate their own ideas about a story the map might be telling. For example, you might explain how the design on the map reminds you of a quilt and makes you think the people are all different, just like the materials are all different; but, they are sewn together tightly. This might suggest the people are connected, possibly through their shared experience of living in Africa. This should spur a conversation about how people can be so different and so close together at the same time and act as a springboard to forming a story about the map.

Write (What are some examples of ways humans interact with their environment that could be included within the study of geography?)

Your student might have difficulty coming up with ideas and may benefit from hearing your ideas first. An idea to get them started could be that humans build dams to get electricity and water. This involves the physical feature of a river. Ask your student to think about other physical features in their community that they may interact with or see others interact with, such as trees being cut down to make new houses in a neighborhood.

Read (Using Maps to Tell Stories)

Help your student understand the concept of a map telling a story by explaining that people can use the information they learn from a map to better understand an area. People can select different types of print media about a subject area, such as magazines, reference books, and historical fiction novels to learn different things about the subject from each source. Likewise, people can learn different information from different maps of an area. This information can then be put together to form a "story" about the area.

Practice

Guide your student to observe the colors on the physical map first, such as asking what the darker brown color on the map means (higher elevation). Highlight the countries and oceans labeled in the second map. Additionally, point to the different icons on the second map that tell more about the country, such as how the pictures of camels show animals that live in the country. Encourage your student to examine a certain area shown on both maps and discuss what they can learn about the same area by looking at each map. For example, the lighthouse is shown on the second map. On the first map, that area is green meaning it is at a low elevation closer to sea level. This makes sense since a lighthouse is often located near a large body of water.

Extension Activity

Country Study

Your student will pick a country to study in each unit throughout this course. They will be given tasks each chapter for the country they chose that coincide with the lesson objectives. For this lesson, they have two tasks: 1) to find multiple maps of your country and write about the story they think those maps are telling and 2) to create a map for the country they chose and write the story their map tells about their country.

For example, they might select the country of Ethiopia. They might draw a map that shows lakes and rivers, as well as where cities are located. Then they might write something like this:

"Ethiopia is not on the coast, so all of its water comes from lakes, rivers, and rain. It has a lot of lakes and rivers. It probably doesn't get a lot of rain. The cities are mostly located in the green areas or near water. I'm guessing the cities are near water because people like to live near water. I don't really know why cities are in the green areas yet."

They might also look at maps of Ethiopia that show migrations of people throughout history or the animal and plants common to the country. As your student looks at the maps, guide them to think about what information they are learning from the maps. Have them point to colors, symbols, or textures on the maps and identify what they mean. To help formulate a story, ask your student to think about what they would tell another person about the maps. How would they describe the country to someone who couldn't see the maps?

Learning Styles

Auditory learners may enjoy listening to the correct pronunciations of some of the countries in Africa. These pronunciations can be found online. Additionally, your student may enjoy listening to an "audio map" of some sounds of Africa. Try searching for "natural sounds of Africa."

Visual learners may enjoy constructing maps of the same location but showing different things. They can try mapping their home (or bedroom) but telling a different story with each map.

Kinesthetic learners may enjoy going out into the community to observe human interaction with the environment and sharing their observations with you verbally or in writing.

Extension Activities

Make a Physical Map
Have your student make a physical map. Physical maps can be made using clay (packaged or homemade) and food coloring or pastels. They could make a map of Africa using the physical maps in the lesson as a model, or they could make a map of their own state or community. Use the clay to mold various physical features and the food coloring or pastels to add more detail to the map.

My Ideal Community
Your student could draw a map of the community they created in the In the Real World section in the worktext to show its physical or cultural geography.

Answer Key

Write (*What can these maps tell you about the physical features of Africa?*)
Answers may vary. Possible answers: The shape of Africa is wider at the top and narrower at the bottom. There is an island off the southeastern coast. There is a dark green color in the middle of Africa. This land might be good for farming.

Write (*What are some examples of ways humans interact with their environment that could be included within the study of geography?*)
Answers will vary. Possible answers:

Human-Environment Interaction	Physical Feature Involved
I like to go fishing.	Water (rivers, lakes, oceans)
I like to grow and harvest crops.	Land suitable for this purpose
I like to go hiking.	Mountains

Practice

Answers will vary. Possible answers:

Map on left: There are a lot of high elevation areas that are probably really dry, and it might be cold. The only low elevation areas are along the coast. There is very little water inside the country.

Map on right: Visitors can go sailing or visit the mountains. There is a castle to visit on the coastline. There are camels all over the country.

Story: The coastline might be a nice place to visit, especially in the north, as there are palm trees and sailing. According to the one map, the mountains look like they get snow, which surprises me! I wonder what the low elevations are like where the camels also live.

Show What You Know

1. A

2. physical, cultural

3. (a) C
   (b) P
   (c) P
   (d) C

4. Answers will vary. Possible answer: This map is telling the story of the cities and physical geography of Egypt. It shows that the cities are located on the coastline or in the green area of the map. The map also tells me that there are some areas of higher elevation in Egypt, but there are not big cities located there. Egypt is on the edge of the Sahara Desert. These areas are probably really hot during the day and might get cold at night. I would need to know more about this, but it doesn't sound like a place people would want to live.

Lesson Objectives

By the end of this lesson, your student will be able to:

- analyze geographic factors that influence where people live in Africa
- identify the significance of key physical features of Africa

Supporting Your Student

Explore

Help your student get excited for this lesson by pulling up a topographical map of their hometown on the computer. Look at the different physical features that are in or near your hometown. These may include mountains, rivers, plateaus, plains, or lakes. Ask your student why they think their town was settled near these physical features. Ask, "How do the physical features contribute to the town?" or "Why do you think people want to live close to these physical features?"

Read

After each section that your student reads, ask them which physical feature they read about. Ask them what the characteristics of the physical feature are. Then ask, "Why would people want to or not want to live near this physical feature? How would it help or hinder them?" This will help solidify your student's understanding of how physical features influence where people live in Africa.

Practice

Help your student fill out the graphic organizer by having a discussion about what the importance of the first physical feature is. Ask, "Why are rivers important to people? How do they help them to survive?" When your student has a good idea about why rivers are important, have them write their ideas down. If they are struggling, ask them to return to the "Rivers" section in the lesson to reread.

Learning Styles

Auditory learners may enjoy discussing the importance of each of the geographical features in Africa and the benefits and disadvantages of living near them.

Visual learners may enjoy creating a map or drawing of the different physical features and labeling it with the reasons they are significant.

Kinesthetic learners may enjoy creating three-dimensional representations of each of the physical features either with paper or other art supplies.

Extension Activities

Let's Explore

Take a field trip either on foot or in the car around your hometown or the surrounding area. Bring a topographical map of the area with you and work with your student to point out each of the different geographical features in your area.

Chart It out

Create a poster size chart with your student of each of the physical features that were covered in the lesson. Print out a picture of each of the features and label them with their name and their important characteristics. Put the chart on the wall for future reference.

Answer Key

Explore

Answers will vary depending on your student's selection.

Write (Why do people choose to settle near the rainforest and the savanna?)

Answers will vary. Possible answer: People choose to settle near the rainforest and the savanna because there is access to food. In the rainforest, animals and plants are available to eat. In the savanna, people can raise livestock and some crops.

Write (Why would people choose to live on the coast rather than in the desert?)

Answers will vary. Possible answer: People would choose to live on the coast rather than in the desert because there is more access to food and water. Life in the desert is much harder than life on the coast.

Practice

Answers may vary. Possible answers:

Physical Features	Importance
Rivers	Rivers supply food and water to people living near them. They are also good places to farm.
Mountains	Mountains provide a little bit cooler climate for the people living near or on them. When the snow melts off of them, it supplies rivers with water.
Savannas	The savanna provides people with animals to eat. It also provides their livestock with grass to feed on.
Deserts	Deserts are dry places where it is very difficult to live. Most people choose not to settle here.
Lakes	Lakes provide people with water and food sources. They also feed important rivers like the Nile.
Coasts	The coast provides people with food and trade opportunities.
Rainforests	The rainforest provides people with access to water and food sources.

Show What You Know

1. A
2. A
3. A, C
4. B, C
5. False
6. True
7. False
8. True
9. True
10. False

Lesson Objectives

By the end of this lesson, your student will be able to:

- compare and contrast human settlements in different regions in Africa
- analyze how the environment influenced settlements in Africa

Supporting Your Student

Read

After your student finishes the sections entitled "People of the Serengeti" and "Desert People," ask, "What similarities do you see between the settlements in the Serengeti and the Sahara Desert?" Reinforce the idea that the settlements are nomadic and that the people build temporary shelters so they can follow their herds to different pastures. Talk to your student about why it is important for the people living in these regions to be able to move quickly. You will want to make sure they understand that the people need to be able to move quickly in order to find food and water for themselves and their animals.

Write *(What similarities or differences do you see between people living in the desert and people living near rivers?)*

Help your student compare and contrast the settlements in the desert with those near the rivers by showing them how to create a Venn diagram. In one circle, write *desert*. In the other, write *rivers*, and have your student write down the unique characteristics of the settlements from each region under the appropriate heading. In the middle, your student will write the similarities between the two. Once your student has a good idea of the similarities and differences between the settlements in these two regions, they are ready to write.

Practice

Help your student with this activity by directing them to reread the section pertaining to each region, looking for clues about what the different settlements look like. Have them start with the "People of the Serengeti" section and ask them to underline all the details that help them to visualize what a settlement there might look like. Once they are done, have them draw the settlement based on the details in the text.

Learning Styles

Auditory learners may enjoy listening to a podcast about the Maasai or the Bedouins.

Visual learners may enjoy watching a video about life on the Serengeti and comparing the information in the video to what they have read in the lesson.

Kinesthetic learners may enjoy building replicas of the different settlements in the Serengeti, Sahara, on the coasts, and near rivers.

Extension Activities

Foldable

Help your student fold a piece of paper into fourths. At the top of the sections, ask your student to write the different regions covered in the chapter: Serengeti, desert, coast, and rivers. Have your student list the characteristics of the environment found in each region.

Connections to Home

Discuss the environment of your hometown with your student. Ask your student how the environment in which you live influences the way that people have settled. What kinds of homes are built? What kinds of jobs do people do that are dependent upon the environment? Have your student write their ideas down on a piece of paper.

Answer Key

Explore

Answers will vary. Possible answer: The capital cities are located near rivers or coastal areas.

Write (*What similarities or differences do you see between people living in the desert and people living near rivers?*)

Answers will vary. Possible answers:

The settlements in the desert and near rivers are different because in the desert, the settlements are temporary and can be easily moved, while the settlements near rivers are permanent.

People in both of the regions settle in ways that allow them to find food and water in order to survive.

Practice

Region	Settlement
Serengeti	Homes are round and made of mud, cow dung, and grasses. They are temporary and do not last for a long time. Cattle are present and important.
Desert	Homes are tents and can be easily moved. There will be camels around.
River	The settlements are permanent. There will be farms present and fishing boats.
Coast	Cities are found here. Tall permanent buildings and houses are present, and there might be a seaport for shipping and trading.

Show What You Know

1. A, B
2. D
3. A, C
4. A
5. B
6. A

Lesson Objectives

By the end of this lesson, your student will be able to:

- describe how natural resources influenced the development of various African civilizations

Supporting Your Student

Explore
Help your student get ready for this lesson by discussing the natural resources that are found around your hometown with them. Talk to them about how the natural resources that are important to your hometown influence the town. For example, if you live near an oil field, it is likely that some of the people living in the town work in the oil industry. This will help your student to understand how natural resources in Africa influenced the development of the different civilizations there.

Read (Ancient Egypt)
After your student reads this section, talk to them about how the flooding of the Nile deposited rich soils on the banks of the river. The soils came from the Mediterranean Sea and made the soil near the Nile River extremely fertile. Your student may not understand why this is important, so try to explain that these soils were like fertilizer for the crops and made them grow in abundance. This allowed the Egyptians to feed more people, and the civilization grew strong as a result.

Practice
Help your student with this section by discussing the importance of rivers with them. They will most likely mention the Nile, but be sure to reiterate that other rivers were also used for trade routes. These trade routes were very important to African civilizations because they facilitated trade between the civilizations. Once your student understands the importance of rivers, ask them to fill in the graphic organizer and move to the next natural resource.

Learning Styles

Auditory learners may enjoy creating a podcast about the importance of natural resources on the development of civilizations in Africa. They can then listen to their podcast.

Visual learners may enjoy creating a natural resource map for Africa. They can find where each civilization in Africa was and create symbols to show which resources were important for them.

Kinesthetic learners may enjoy looking at and touching a small piece of gold or gold jewelry and then explaining how gold was important in influencing the development of different civilizations in Africa.

Extension Activities

Close to Home
With your student, perform an internet search on the capital city of your home country. Look up which natural resources were important in the development of that city. Discuss this information with your student and ask how this affected the development of the country as a whole.

Natural Resource or Not?
Gather together a bunch of different objects. This should include objects that are completely man-made and objects that are made of natural resources. Jumble the objects together and ask your student to sort them into natural resources versus man-made objects. Discuss the difference with your student after they are finished.

Answer Key

Explore

Answers will vary. Possible answers: They were able to trade with other countries or had valuable resources, such as gold and diamonds.

Write *(Which natural resource helped both the ancient Mali civilization and the ancient Egyptian civilization grow?)*

Answers may vary. Possible answer: Rivers helped both the ancient Mali and ancient Egyptian civilizations. The Nile River helped provide fertile soil for ancient Egyptians to grow crops. The ancient Mali civilization used rivers to easily transport gold for trading.

Write *(List the natural resources that influenced the development of the different civilizations in Africa.)*

Answers may vary. Possible answers: rivers, rich soil, gold, grasslands, ocean

Practice

Natural Resource	How It Influenced the Different Civilizations
Rivers	Rivers helped ancient Egypt grow because of the rich soil that was deposited. Rivers helped the Mali civilization because they created trade routes for trading gold.
Gold	Gold was important to Mali and Great Zimbabwe. It made them grow rich through trade.
Oceans	The ocean was very important for ancient Carthage because it allowed them to control the trade routes between Europe and Africa.
Grasslands	The grasslands were important for Great Zimbabwe because they allowed them to graze their cattle.

Show What You Know

1. B
2. A
3. D
4. C
5. C
6. A
7. D
8. True
9. True
10. False

Lesson Objectives

By the end of this lesson, your student will be able to:

- identify ways that people in Africa made changes to their environment and how they responded to changes in the environment
- explain the significance of the Suez Canal to Africa and the world

Supporting Your Student

Explore
Help your student get ready for the lesson by discussing the environment of your hometown with them. You will want to talk about whether you have a dry or wet climate, the average temperatures, and the differences between the seasons. Then help your student think about the ways that people in your hometown have adapted to or changed the environment in order to survive there. Maybe your house has air conditioning for the hot summer months or people have very warm clothes for when it gets cold. This discussion will help your student begin to understand that people change and adapt to their environments in Africa.

Read (Deforestation)
Your student may be saddened by the deforestation that is taking place in the rainforest in Africa. Help them to understand why people need to cut down the trees by discussing what the trees are used for. Help build empathy by talking to your student about the lives of the people living around the rainforest. Reiterate that often the people living here are very poor and do not have access to other forms of energy.

Read (Suez Canal)
To help your student better understand the importance of the Suez Canal, pull up a map of the canal online. It may also be helpful to pull up a map of trade routes before the Canal was built and afterward. Discuss how much shorter the route through the canal is compared to the route that goes around the southern tip of Africa.

Learning Styles

Auditory learners may enjoy listening to recorded sounds of the rainforest in the Congo River Basin.

Visual learners may enjoy creating a map of the old trade routes around the southern tip of Africa and the newer route through the Suez Canal.

Kinesthetic learners may enjoy building a replica of the Suez Canal with art supplies or pillows and pretending to be a ship captain navigating through the canal.

Extension Activities

Save the Rainforest
With your student, brainstorm some ways to save the rainforest from deforestation. After you have brainstormed, have your student create a pamphlet that can be handed out to educate others about ways to save the rainforest.

Irrigation Station
Find a sandbox or a patch of dirt outside. Have your student build a trench that replicates a river. Then show them how to build little offshoots from the river to replicate irrigation ditches. Pour water into the main river trench and watch as it goes into the irrigation trenches. Discuss with your student how this would help farmers grow crops in arid places.

Answer Key

Explore

Answers will vary depending on your student's environment. Possible answers: People have built man-made lakes and rivers, dams, and bridges across larger bodies of water.

Write *(How do the people in Egypt and the Democratic Republic of Congo change their environments in order to survive?)*

Answers may vary. Possible answers: In Egypt, people create irrigation systems tied to the Nile to water their crops. In the Democratic Republic of Congo, people cut down the rainforest to make room for roads and mines.

Write *(List four ways that people change their environment in Africa.)*

Answers may vary. Possible answers: irrigation, deforestation, urbanization, building the Suez Canal

Practice

Drawings will vary. Possible answers:

- urbanization: the process of making an area into a city
- deforestation: the cutting down of large groups of trees or forests
- agriculture: the practice of farming
- irrigation: the process of bringing water to places where it does not usually flow

Show What You Know

1. C
2. B, C
3. B
4. C
5. C
6. A

Lesson Objectives

By the end of this lesson, your student will be able to:

• identify key natural resources found in Africa

Supporting Your Student

Take a Closer Look (Natural Resource Map in Africa)

To help your student better understand how natural resources are distributed throughout Africa, have them track the resources on the map found on the last page of the lesson. Throughout the lesson, your student will color this map according to the key. Help your student color these countries in as they read so they will have a completed map at the end of the lesson. Discuss how natural resources are distributed in Africa. Ask them if they notice any patterns.

Read

After your student reads these sections, help them find a video that further explains how gold, diamonds, platinum, and cobalt are distributed. This will give them a visual of how these resources are created and why they are concentrated in certain areas in Africa and across the globe. In general, areas with a lot of volcanic activity, tectonic plate shifting, etc. tend to provide the intense heat and pressure needed to create many of these natural resources.

Practice

If your student created the colorful map throughout the lesson, they may be able to fill this chart in fairly easily. If not, help your student go back to each of the sections and find the names of the countries or regions where each natural resource is found. It may be helpful to pull up a map of Africa and point out each of the different countries.

Learning Styles

Auditory learners may enjoy discussing the patterns they notice about the distribution of natural resources in Africa with you.

Visual learners may enjoy drawing a visual glossary of the natural resources found in Africa. They could draw a picture of each resource, give a description of how it is used, and list where the resource is found in Africa.

Kinesthetic learners may enjoy building a three-dimensional map out of clay to show where each of the natural resources is located throughout Africa. They could shape the continent out of the clay and then include three-dimensional elements or carve designs into the different regions to represent where various natural resources are found.

Extension Activities

Dig It

Bury some coins in a box of sand or dirt. Ask your student how they could find them without just digging up the entire box of sand or dirt. Explain that when people are looking for natural resources found underground, they often have to come up with processes like this in order to find them because they cannot just dig up huge areas of land in search of the resource. Research how people find resources, such as using sonar or other types of imaging that map beneath Earth's surface.

Gold Rush

Take your student to an area where there is running water. Bring a strainer with very small holes in it. Instruct your student to scoop up a little bit of sediment and then shake it so the water and tiny pieces fall out. Your student should then look through the pieces to see if they find any gold. They might find some minerals that look like gold. Tell your student that this is how many people who are looking for gold spend their days. Discuss how they would like to have this for a job.

Answer Key

Explore

Answers will vary. Possible answers: fish, water, sand for making glass, clams

Write *(Which geologic process is responsible for distributing diamonds, platinum, and gold on the African continent?)*

Answers may vary. Possible answer: Volcanic processes are responsible for the distribution of diamonds, platinum, and gold on the African continent.

Practice

Natural Resource	Country or Region
Diamonds	Botswana, Angola, Democratic Republic of Congo, South Africa, and Namibia
Platinum	South Africa, Ghana, Mali, and Tanzania
Gold	South Africa, Ghana, Mali, and Tanzania
Cobalt	Democratic Republic of Congo
Fish	Somalia, Eritrea, Kenya, and Djibouti Coasts of Western Africa
Forests	Central and Western Africa

Show What You Know

1. B
2. E
3. A
4. True
5. True
6. False
7. True

Lesson Objectives

By the end of this lesson, your student will be able to:

- identify key natural resources found in Africa
- describe the use, distribution, and importance of natural resources and how they can affect different groups in Africa
- describe the impact of trade on the availability of natural resources throughout Africa

Supporting Your Student

Read (Natural Resources of Africa)
It may be helpful to have a physical map of Africa on hand when your student is reading about the key natural resources that are available in Africa and the geographic locations that they are found in. For example, as your student reads about the use, distribution, and importance of Africa's natural resources, they could point out where these natural resources are produced and how they may impact trade to neighboring regions.

Write (How can the use and distribution of natural resources affect groups of people in Africa?)
Help your student generate their response to this question by asking them to think about how the different groups mentioned in the lesson rely on the resources around them to survive. For example, some groups like the Bedouins have to move around a lot to find the best conditions for raising livestock and growing crops. They rely on those plants and animals to survive.

Practice
Assist your student in completing the bubble map by breaking up the task into smaller sections and focusing on the connections between the topics shown on the various bubbles. For example, first ask your student to identify the natural resources of Africa. Then, ask your student to identify how that resource is used by people inside and outside of Africa. Finally, discuss what impacts the trading of that resource may have. For example, timber is a natural resource found in Africa. It is used for building things.

When trees are cut down to be sold as part of trade, the trees are not available for people and animals in the area who need them. Having less trees can also hurt the environment.

Learning Styles

Auditory learners may enjoy listening to how the names of natural resources are pronounced in different African languages.

Visual learners may enjoy making a collage on Africa's diverse natural resources and how they are used within the continent and around the world.

Kinesthetic learners may enjoy examining the textures of natural metals such as silver, gold, diamond, and iron. You might have items in your household that are made of these elements, or you may be able to examine them at a local store or museum.

Extension Activities

Museum Tour of Africa
With your student, take a trip to the Natural History Museum to gather information on African tribes, available natural resources, and trade routes. Have your student compare how each tribe differs from one another based on the regions of Africa they live in and if the demand for natural resources outweighs their availability.

Create Your Own Jewelry!
Have your student design jewelry pieces using beads, gems, or rhinestones to depict natural metals found in Africa (if items made of these elements are not available at home). For example, your student may be interested in creating a diamond and gold necklace. As your student designs the necklace, discuss the size, weight (in karats), and potential cost of the jewelry by investigating the recommended price per karat for diamond and gold.

Answer Key

Explore

Answers will vary. Possible answers: diamonds and gold are important because people can sell them for a lot of money and make jewelry with them, iron is important because people can make things like tools from it

Write *(What are the two most profitable mineral resources in Africa?)*

Diamonds and gold

Write *(How can the use and distribution of natural resources affect groups of people in Africa?)*

Answers will vary. Possible answers: Water and food are scarce in the dry Sahara Desert so groups have to move around to find resources to grow crops and raise livestock. Groups can hunt animals and gather food around them to survive.

Practice

Answers will vary. Possible answers:

Types of Natural Resources: gold, diamonds, iron, uranium, nickel, ivory, timber, plants for medicine

How the Resources Are Used: to make jewelry, magnets, coins, batteries, drill bits, timber for building, medicine

How Trade Affects Natural Resources: can endanger a population of animals like elephants, may hurt the environment as people remove the resources to sell which affects other natural resources like plants and animals, resources that are traded are not available for people in the area to use, people can get resources from other areas that they may not have

Show What You Know

1. A, B, C, D
2. gold, diamonds
3. A
4. D
5. Possible answers: As people trade natural resources, there may be less available for people to use in a certain area. Animal populations, like the elephant, can become endangered. People can get different natural resources that they might not have available in their area.

Lesson Objectives

By the end of this lesson, your student will be able to:

- describe how cultural attitudes, political unrest, economic downturns, or natural disasters influenced the behavior of people in an area of Africa
- identify an example of voluntary and involuntary human migration in Africa
- identify examples of the influences and contributions migrants can bring to the new region where they settled

Supporting Your Student

Explore

If your student feels that they really don't know much about Africa, you may want to discuss what you know about Africa or have your student watch a documentary online about Africa.

Some of the facts to share could include:

- Africa is a continent and not a country.
- Many African countries have had struggling economies throughout the years.
- There have been many civil wars in several African countries because they fought over natural resources.

Read

Since your student will be discussing the different areas and countries of Africa, it might be beneficial for your student to practice identifying where the countries are located in Africa. You can practice or quiz your student by using a paper or online map of Africa. Point to a country on the map and have your student guess the country. As your student reads about different countries throughout the lesson, they can refer to the map to see where they are found.

Write *(Explain how the natural resources helped and hurt the countries in Africa.)*

Look up how much diamonds, gold, and oil cost today. Share this information with your student. Then, discuss why these things are so valuable to people around the world. This can help your student see why many people may want to mine and sell the natural resources in Africa.

Practice

While reading the text with your student, you may want to discuss the cause of certain events from the Read section that took place and the effects that took place as a result. For example, you may want to ask, "What caused people to move to the Ivory Coast for jobs?" (the discovery of oil).

Learning Styles

Auditory learners may enjoy watching documentaries or having a discussion about how natural resources have positively and negatively impacted Africa.

Visual learners may enjoy using a blank map of Africa and color-coordinating the map according to the natural resources found in various areas of Africa, countries that have fought in civil wars or had conflicts, and areas where the land is mainly used for agriculture and farming.

Kinesthetic learners may enjoy building a garden and growing a few vegetables. Your student will begin to understand how difficult it is to grow their own food. In the worktext, your student learned that many African families farm their own land through subsistence farming. They grow enough food to feed their families, but not much more.

Extension Activities

Research A Country

Have your student choose a country from Africa. Research online about that country by answering the following questions.

1. Which country did you pick?
2. What natural resources are found in this country?
3. Did your country have any events in the past, such as political unrest or natural disasters, that caused people to migrate? Explain.
4. Do you think people migrated to this country or away from this country? Explain.

After conducting the research, have your student create a poster by drawing a picture of the country with the natural resources on it. Also include images that depict the problems experienced by the African people.

Compare and Contrast Farming

There are two types of farming—subsistence farming and commercial farming. Have your student look up the definitions of both of these types of farming. Think about what is needed for each type of farming. Investigate why families may have to migrate away from their subsistence or commercial farmland and where they could go. Would it be in the same country or region?

Answer Key

Explore

All answers could potentially be correct. Possible answers: to mine for diamonds and gold, to move from rural areas to urban areas for jobs, to move to safer regions away from violence, to move away from areas affected by natural disasters

Write *(Explain how the natural resources helped and hurt the countries in Africa.)*

Answers may vary. Possible answers: Several African countries had discovered diamond and gold mines and oil. Sierra Leone, the Democratic Republic of the Congo, and Liberia found diamonds and gold, whereas the Ivory Coast discovered oil. This allowed the countries to export these valuable products to other countries outside of Africa or companies within Africa. However, it caused many problems including civil wars between groups fighting for the valuable natural resources.

Practice

Answers may vary. Possible answers:

Cause	Effect
People heard about jobs in tourism and business.	People began to move to major cities.
Diamonds were discovered and mined in Africa.	Money from diamond sales were used to hurt or harm other people.
Civil wars and conflicts happened in a country.	People had to involuntarily migrate.
The Ivory Coast discovered oil.	Many people moved to the Ivory Coast for jobs.
Floods, droughts, and famines happen.	People had to involuntarily migrate.

Show What You Know

1. B
2. C
3. A
4. Answers may vary. Possible answer: People in Africa migrated to areas in Africa, and they moved away from areas of Africa for different reasons. People can migrate to an area where natural resources are found. They want to mine for those resources. These people moved voluntarily because they had the choice to better their lives. When violence erupts in countries, people can move away from those countries to safer regions of Africa. They moved involuntarily due to being forced to move to another area in order for their families to be safe. People who had settled for generations in certain regions of Africa may find that they need to move elsewhere. These families would farm the land to feed their families. The land may not be able to produce crops anywhere due to flooding, drought, or famine.

Lesson Objectives

By the end of this lesson, your student will be able to:

- identify cultural features found in Africa
- describe how cultural features in a region of Africa influence factors of daily life, such as the economy, government, or transportation

Supporting Your Student

Read *(Food)*

As your student reads about the cultural features of food, it may be helpful to have a physical map of Africa available to help your student point out geographic regions where staple crops are grown. You may also wish to incorporate a map that details the climates of Africa to give your student a frame of reference. For example, the climate of East Africa varies between cool and moist to warm and dry conditions. Yams, which are a major food source for the region, thrive successfully here as they grow best in moist and warm climates. Climate conditions can be easily pointed out on a climate map, as they showcase color. Typically, the more orange or red a region is, the hotter and drier the area. The bluer or greener a region is, the cooler and wetter the area.

Read *(Religion)*

Remind your student that religion can influence a number of different areas of daily life outside of the examples mentioned in the worktext. Deeply held religious beliefs can influence everything from what a person eats to their family size and roles, daily schedule, and how they utilize their resources such as money. In Africa, many tribes and people groups have practiced religious beliefs specific to their culture for thousands of years. Over time, many people have either converted to worldwide religions like Christianity or Islam or mixed some of their traditional beliefs with the beliefs of these religions.

It's important for your student to recognize that in Africa, like other places around the world, religion can be a divisive and sensitive topic within cultures. People can be persecuted or discriminated against for their religious beliefs, which can influence how they live. Additionally, if people of a certain religion are in power in government, they might also impose rules or laws that can be unfair to people of other faiths.

Practice

To assist your student with this activity, ask guiding questions to help them identify an example of a cultural feature in Africa and how it might influence daily life. For example, your student may want to focus on food. First, you could ask them to identify an example of food associated with a particular culture in Africa, such as yams. Then, you could ask your student how this food source influences what people do for jobs. In this case, people in the areas where yams are grown often work as farmers.

Learning Styles

Auditory learners may enjoy listening to recordings of different languages spoken in Africa or music played from different geographical regions.

Visual learners may enjoy watching a video on how different African art was created. Encourage your student to describe any unique tools or materials used to create the art piece.

Kinesthetic learners may enjoy creating hand motions or body movements for the types of cultural features. For example, for art, they may pretend to paint something.

Extension Activities

Make an African Dish!

With your student, research popular African food recipes that can be easily created, such as West African sweet potato stew, Qumbe (East African coconut candy), or Moroccon vegetable soup. As your student makes the dish, discuss the taste, smell, and feel of the ingredients and the technique(s) used to make the recipe. Compare these findings to your student's favorite food. How are they similar or different?

Learn an African Language

With your student, learn key phrases in commonly spoken African languages such as Swahili, Hausa, or Yoruba by perusing language software programs or looking for videos. As your student pronounces each word, discuss the alphabet system that is used and any unique features of the language, such as the syntax or the arrangement of words to form a sentence.

Answer Key

Explore
Answers will vary. Possible answers: They all look like they are carved. There are carvings of people on them. They can tell us something about each tribe or culture.

Write (What is one way religion, beliefs, and values influence how people live in Africa?)
Answers may vary. Possible answers: Religion, beliefs, and values can influence how laws are made and communities interact with each other. They can also influence the types of jobs people have.

Practice
Answers may vary. Possible answers:

Cultural Features	Examples in Africa	How does it influence how people live?
food	Yams, plantains, and cassavas are grown in many places on the continent. Nomads in Sub-Saharan Africa raise livestock as a food source.	Many people work as farmers, and a lot of the economy is based on farming. Nomads use camels to move around in search of water and food for their livestock.
language	Many languages are spoken across Africa. Swahili is the official language of Kenya.	Countries often have an official language so people can speak a common language. People in Kenya often have to know Swahili to do business and fill out documents.
religion	Christianity, Islam, and other traditional religions are practiced.	Laws and community rules can be influenced by what popular religious groups think is appropriate.
beliefs and values	Farming communities in Sub-Saharan Africa have many of the same beliefs, including working together as a community.	They work together to protect each other against common enemies or do activities together like hunting.

Show What You Know
1. C, D
2. Answers may vary. Possible answers: art, language, religion, food, music, architecture, clothing, shared beliefs, values
3. Answers may vary. Possible answers:
   - Food: Yams, plantains, and cassavas are grown in many places on the continent. Many people work as farmers, and a lot of the economy is based on farming. Nomads in Sub-Saharan Africa raise livestock as a food source, so they use camels to move around in search of water and food for their livestock.
   - Languages: Many languages are spoken across Africa, which means countries often have an official language so people can speak a common language. Swahili is the official language of Kenya, so people in Kenya often have to know Swahili to do business and fill out documents.
   - Religion: Christianity, Islam, and other traditional religions are practiced, so laws and community rules can be influenced by what popular religious groups think is appropriate.
   - Beliefs and Values: Farming communities in Sub-Saharan Africa have many of the same beliefs, including working together as a community. This leads them to work together to protect each other against common enemies or do activities together like hunting.

LESSON 10
Cultural Geography of Africa

Lesson Objectives

By the end of this lesson, your student will be able to:

- describe the cultural geography of different regions in Africa
- identify influences of African culture on individuals and civilizations around the world

Supporting Your Student

Read *(Musical Instruments)*

It may be helpful to refer to the images of African instruments, such as the talking and djembe, when reading so your student is able to visualize the differences between these instruments. With your student, you can also research how these instruments are played. If your student has access to drums nearby, your student can compare and contrast the structure, sound, and playing method of these instruments.

Read *(Architecture)*

As your student reads through this section of text, it may be helpful to have samples of stone or granite available for your student to touch and assess the look, texture, size, and weight of these rocks. If geological rock samples are not available, encourage your student to research these types of rock to better understand the materials that were used to build ancient architecture such as the pyramids of Egypt and the Roman Colosseum in Rome.

Write *(How have cultures in Africa influenced science, technology, or architecture around the world?)*

Assist your student in generating a response by relating some of these achievements, such as the Gregorian calendar, to personal life. Encourage your student to think about the following questions: "What might happen if calendars did not exist?" or "How might that affect the way people live?"

Learning Styles

Auditory learners may enjoy listening to recordings of music that highlight the differences in sound among the types of drums played throughout Africa, such as the talking drum and djembe of West Africa and the water drums of Central Africa.

Visual learners may enjoy drawing pictures of the pyramids or stelae to visualize these types of architecture.

Kinesthetic learners may enjoy making models or replicas of famous African architecture such as the pyramids of Egypt or the stelae of Ethiopia from common household items. As your student builds these replicas, discuss the designing and building challenges that ancient architects may have encountered.

Extension Activities

Make Your Own Water Drum!

Water drums are a very old percussion instrument traditionally played among African tribes in Central Africa. With your student, research the materials needed to create a personalized water drum. Some of these materials include bowls, rubber bands, wooden clothespin, sticks, wire (to make a coil), and water. This simple activity can help your student better understand the cultural traditions of instrument making among tribes in Central Africa.

Compare Calendars

With your student, compare the three main types of calendars that are used in the world such as the lunar calendar, solar calendar, and lunisolar calendar. Encourage your student to identify unique features of each calendar system and investigate which civilizations or regions in the world they are used in.

Answer Key

Explore
Answers will vary.

Write (When might people in Africa create music using drums?)
Answers may vary. Possible answers: The people of Africa might create music using drums during weddings, baptisms, and funerals. They might also play them while taking a journey to the river, washing clothes, or bathing.

Write (How have cultures in Africa influenced science, technology, or architecture around the world?)
Answers may vary. Possible answers: invention of the Gregorian calendar, charting of the constellations, charting of the moon cycle, use of salicylic acid, use of stone to build, building of tall monuments like stelae

Practice
Answers may vary. Possible answers:

Music: talking drum and djembe from West Africa; mbira from West Africa; influenced jazz, gospel, Cuban, and soul music

Science and Technology: dividing a year into 12 months; charting of sun, constellations, and moon cycles; use of salicylic acid to treat headaches and fevers; influenced the modern-day calendar

Architecture: use of stone to build, building of tall monuments like stelae, influenced Greek and Roman architecture and other monuments

Show What You Know
1. A, B, C, E, F
2. A
3. A, C
4. B
5. C

Lesson Objectives

By the end of this lesson, your student will review the following big ideas from Chapter 1.

- Geographers study both physical and cultural geography. (Lesson 1)
- Africa has many important physical features, including deserts, rainforests, savannas, and rivers. (Lesson 2)
- The environment plays a role where people choose to settle and what their settlements look like. (Lesson 3)
- Natural resources impact where civilizations develop. (Lesson 4)
- People in Africa have changed their environment. (Lesson 5)
- Key natural resources in Africa include gold, platinum, fish, and forests. (Lesson 6)
- Trade can cause a decrease in the availability of natural resources in Africa as many people mine and gather resources to sell, like gold, diamonds, and timber. (Lesson 7)
- Cultural attitudes, political unrest, economic downturns, and natural disasters have influenced the migration of people in Africa. (Lesson 8)
- Cultural features in regions of Africa influence population, the economy, government, and transportation. (Lesson 9)
- The cultural geography of Africa is diverse, and several cultural features differ among regions of the continent. (Lesson 10)

Supporting Your Student

Practice (Visualizing Vocabulary)
Help your student visualize important vocabulary words by encouraging them to think of an image that is best associated with the word. To do this, it would be helpful to have your student look through images that are associated with the word. For example, when defining the word *culture*, your student may think of a favorite food (i.e., pizza) or a favorite example of architecture (i.e., Egyptian pyramids). Encourage your student to draw basic features of both to reinforce

the idea that culture encompasses more than one characteristic.

Practice (Identifying and Understanding Natural Resources)
Help your student complete the table by identifying two key natural resources in Africa. Encourage your student to refer to the corresponding chapter lessons to investigate in which region(s) in Africa these natural resources are found, their uses, and their influence in the world. For example, diamonds are a key natural resource found in countries such as South Africa, the Democratic Republic of Congo, and Namibia. They are predominantly used in jewelry and are exported throughout the world. However, a lot of trees are cut down or the ground is dug up to mine them, which destroys homes for plants and animals while harming the environment.

Practice (Bubble Map)
Assist your student in filling in the bubble map in three basic steps. First, have your student select a region of interest in Africa. Second, ask your student to write down the physical and cultural features of that region, such as mountains, lakes, music, natural resources, or religion. As space permits on the page, have them add more detail about each characteristic they listed. An example can be found in the Answer Key.

Learning Styles

Auditory learners may enjoy discussing the physical and cultural geography of a certain country or region in Africa.

Visual learners may enjoy taking a virtual or in-person trip to a natural history museum or art gallery to learn more about the geographic features of Africa and how culture has influenced both ancient and modern people.

Kinesthetic learners may enjoy filming their own documentary to highlight the key physical and cultural features in Africa.

Extension Activities

Virtual Field Trip

Choose two regions in Africa to explore with your student and take a virtual field trip. Watch videos, explore photographs, and participate in simulations about different regions in Africa. Many online encyclopedias and embassy websites have extensive information about life in different African regions and countries. As your student explores each region, have them keep a journal of their virtual field trip, such as taking notes of the location, climate, physical features, and cultural features.

Guess That Region

Have your student create a drawing of a region in Africa and provide two or three clues about the region without saying its name. Have someone else guess what region they are drawing. Be sure to take turns so that your student can guess as well.

Answer Key

Practice (Visualizing Vocabulary)

Answers will vary. Check your student's definitions and drawings to make sure they relate to one another.

Practice (Identifying and Understanding Natural Resources)

Answers will vary. Possible answers:

Type of Natural Resource: Diamonds		
Location	Use	Influence in Africa and the World
South Africa, the Democratic Republic of Congo, and Namibia	jewelry, cutting tool, medicine	cutting down of trees leads to loss of homes and wildlife, which harms the environment

Type of Natural Resource: Nickel		
Location	Use	Influence in Africa and the World
South Africa, Botswana, and Zimbabwe	stainless steel, magnets, coins, rechargeable batteries	recyclable but can contaminate air, water, and soil; increase in production of technology

Practice (Bubble Map)

Answers will vary. Possible answer:

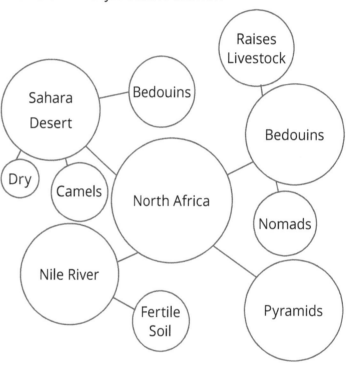

Quick Review

Refer to the statement your student circled in the Show What You Know section to self-assess their knowledge of the chapter concepts. Then to assist in determining if your student is ready to take the assessment, consider:

- Having your student look at a physical map of Africa to identify geographic features, including mountains, rivers, forests, and deserts.
- Having your student explain how the geographical features in regions of the continent influence the people who live there.
- Having your student identify why people migrate in Africa.

Chapter Assessment

Fill in the blanks using the vocabulary words in the Word Bank below.

Word Bank: culture   resources
savanna   desert

2. Religion is an example of _____.

3. As a great place to raise livestock, the _____ is the largest grassland in Africa.

4. Bedouins and other nomads live in the _____, which has dry, arid conditions that cause them to move to find the things they need to survive.

5. Gold, diamonds, nickel, and timber are examples of the types of _____ you would find in Africa.

Circle the correct answer for each question.

6. Which physical features are found in Africa?

A. mountains

B. savannas

C. rainforests

D. deserts

E. all of the above

7. Why do people prefer living on the coast? Circle all correct answers.

A. They have easy access to water for transportation and trade.

B. It is dry and sandy.

C. There is an abundance of fish for eating.

8. How have people in Africa changed their environment? Circle all correct answers.

A. They created irrigation systems for crops.

B. They built the Great Wall to protect themselves from invaders.

C. They created the Suez Canal to ship goods between Europe and Asia.

D. They cut down trees in the Congo River Basin to sell and to burn for energy.

Read each sentence. Circle True or False.

9. True or False   People in Africa might migrate because of a natural disaster or civil wars being fought in their country.

10. True or False   People only migrate involuntarily.

11. True or False   Diamonds, gold, and oil are all important natural resources of Africa.

12. True or False   People in Africa are more likely to make a permanent settlement where they have to travel far for food and water.

Chapter Assessment Answer Key

1. culture
2. savanna
3. desert
4. resources
5. E
6. A, C
7. A, C, D
8. True
9. False
10. True
11. False

Alternative Assessment

Project: Infographic

Project Requirements or Steps:

You will create an infographic to show features of a region in Africa. An infographic is a chart or diagram used to convey information or data quickly and clearly. Use the following steps to create your infographic.

2. Select a region you studied in the chapter. Gather information about the features of this region, including:

   A. physical features

   B. culture

   C. natural resources

   D. migration

3. Create a title for your infographic related to the topic.

4. Include photos and drawings related to the topic.

5. Include information or data to explain and support the photos and drawings you included.

6. Present the information in a creative way.

Alternative Assessment Rubric

Use the following rubric to grade your student's assessment.

	4	3	2	1	Points
Connection to the Chapter	The infographic is clearly connected to the chapter.	The infographic is connected to the chapter.	The infographic is somewhat connected to the chapter.	The infographic is not related to the chapter.	
Creativity	The infographic is very creative and aesthetically appealing.	The infographic is creative and aesthetically appealing.	The infographic is somewhat creative and aesthetically appealing.	The infographic is not creative or aesthetically appealing.	
Information	The information or data is very accurate and easy to follow.	The information or data is accurate.	The information or data is somewhat accurate.	The information or data is not accurate.	
Grammar and Mechanics	There are no grammar or punctuation mistakes.	There are one or two grammar or punctuation mistakes.	There are several grammar or punctuation mistakes.	There are a distracting number of grammar or punctuation mistakes.	

Total Points _____/16

Average _____

Lesson Objectives

By the end of this lesson, your student will be able to:

- examine different maps of Asia and distinguish between political geography, physical geography, and cultural geography
- determine the story that each map tells

Supporting Your Student

Read

Support your student during the Read sections by asking them clarifying questions, including "What would you expect to see on a cultural map?," "What does a physical map tell you about a place?," and "How could a geographer use a political map?" Guide your student to see that a cultural map will focus more on aspects like landmarks, food, activities, and animals. A physical map shows more about the land and water in an area, while a political map shows the borders of countries and the locations of cities.

Write (What story can you tell about China from the maps? What information did you learn?)

Support your student by asking them what story they think each of the maps tells. Ask them how those small stories might work together to create a larger, more in-depth story of China. Encourage them to use clues from the maps to make inferences and to include those ideas in their stories. You might want to guide them to look at the landmarks and where they are located. For example, point out that there appears to be a big wall (Great Wall of China) located in the country that is a large tourist attraction. Ask your student to think about why the Chinese might have built this wall. It could also be helpful to point out that China is bordered by an ocean and a giant mountain range. Ask your student what they think life is like for people in those areas while referencing the other maps. For example, a boat is shown in the water on the cultural map. This might mean that in areas near the water, people fish or go sailing.

Practice

To help your student complete the activity, first discuss what they notice about each map. Point out that the first map seems to show a lot of green, tan, and brown, which are often used to tell about the land of an area. Next, guide your student to see that the second map has a lot of lines and colors that divide the country into different sections. Finally, discuss how the last map shows pictures of things that may be found in the country. Have your student refer to the cultural, physical, and political geography sections in the lesson to compare these maps to the maps in each section.

Learning Styles

Auditory learners may enjoy listening to music from different cultures in Asia. Then they could create a cultural map that shows the types of music popular in each country.

Visual learners may enjoy combining the political, physical, and cultural maps of one of the countries in this lesson into one map showing all three types of geography.

Kinesthetic learners may enjoy creating their own maps out of playdough, clay, or paper to create 3D models.

Extension Activities

Border Discussion

Use an online interactive map to examine the border between Pakistan and India. Ask your student to notice the physical features of the border area and discuss why the border might exist there. Ask about the advantages and disadvantages of having a mountain range on the border between two countries.

Telling Stories

Search the internet for a cultural, political, or physical map of your favorite city. Take turns looking at the map with your child and using details from the map to tell stories about the place. For instance, if you pulled up a tourist map of Chicago, you might notice that the Shedd Aquarium and the Field Museum are very close together. A story you might tell about the place would include ideas about how the people of Chicago value science and education.

Answer Key

Explore

Answers may vary. Possible answers: The countries are different sizes and shapes. Some are small and others are large. They might be divided up by where groups of people live. There might be natural features like rivers and mountains to create borders between countries.

Write (How is political geography different from either cultural or physical geography?)

Answers may vary. Possible answers: Political geography is different from cultural geography because it focuses on boundaries between countries, states, and counties and how people in those areas might interact while cultural geography focuses on natural resources, the economy, and religion. It is also different from physical geography, which focuses on studying Earth's surface.

Write (What story can you tell about China from the maps? What information did you learn?)

Answers will vary. Possible answer:

People in China might like to fish or depend on fish to eat because they created many cities near the ocean and rivers. The people built a lot of large buildings and structures perhaps to show their power and might. They created things like huge walls and palaces. Those walls and palaces still exist today!

The people of China value many things. They love panda bears and dragons. As time went on, they created borders around their great nation. Some of the borders were made near mountains and oceans. These might have kept other people from attacking them. The people of China worked hard to make their nation strong and used the physical features around them to their advantage.

Practice

Map	Is it a physical, cultural, or political map?	How do you know?
	Physical	The physical features are shown on the map. The map shows the different elevations. It shows where the ocean is.
	Cultural	This map shows important cultural landmarks and tourist sites.
	Political	This map shows the different states of Japan. The map shows the different regions and their borders.

Show What You Know

Map A	Political	India is broken up into many different areas or states. Each area seems to have at least one big city where people live.
Map B	Cultural	Elephants are important in India. There is a religious statue, which means religion is important to many Indians. Some women in India wear long dresses while men wear a long, white tunic.
Map C	Physical	India has a lot of water around it, so people probably do a lot of fishing and sailing. At the top of India, there is a dark brown section, which means there are mountains nearby.

Lesson Objectives

By the end of this lesson, your student will be able to:

- identify key physical geographic features in Asia
- describe why people may live near a physical feature found in Asia
- identify different regions of Asia on a map

Supporting Your Student

Read

It may be helpful to have a physical map of Asia available for your student to point out physical features they read about on the map. For example, as your student reads about the Himalayan Mountains, they could point to the mountains on the map. Point out that some physical features are easily found on a map because of color or texture that is used to show them. For example, mountains are often darker brown and look bumpy, while oceans and other bodies of water may be colored blue.

Write (Why are cities located near sources of water?)

Assist your student in generating their response to this question by asking, "What do sources of water, like rivers, provide for humans?" Guide your student to reread the last paragraph of the Rivers and River Deltas section and highlight things sources of water can provide humans, such as fish to eat, animals to hunt, water to drink, and a way to travel.

Read (Regions of Asia)

As your student reads this section of text, have them point to each region on the map and say its name aloud. Point out that this is just one way that geographers divide Asia into regions. Some geographers divide Asia into five regions instead of six, while Asia can also be divided into regions based on its climate and its physical features. For example, mountainous areas and areas with grasslands could be considered two different regions, as could climates that are dry and temperate. By grouping countries that are nearer to each other or those that may share physical, cultural, or historic characteristics together, geographers can more easily look for patterns to help make sense of the world around them.

While discussing the physical features of each region, note how some physical features span across different regions or serve as a "border" between them. For example, the Himalayas are found in both East Asia and South Asia. They form a natural border between the two areas. Historically, this physical feature made it more difficult to cross from one area to the other and could have discouraged the movement of people, goods, ideas, and customs between the two areas.

Learning Styles

Auditory learners may enjoy listening to recordings of the different languages spoken in Asia's regions.

Visual learners may enjoy watching a video about different physical features or examining pictures of river valleys, mountains, or steppes. Encourage your student to point out the similarities and differences between the physical features they are seeing.

Kinesthetic learners may enjoy contorting their bodies into the different landforms. They could make mountains, simulate rivers, and show flat grasslands by moving and stretching in different ways.

Extension Activities

Virtual Scavenger Hunt

With your student, take a trip to the library or go on a virtual scavenger hunt to gather more information about one of the physical features in Asia, such as the Eastern Steppe, Asia's rivers and river valleys, or the Himalayan Mountains. Have your student generate a list of questions they would like to know about each physical feature and then search for answers in books, magazines, and online resources.

Compare Continents

Have your student look back to the maps in previous lessons about Africa. Compare the geographic features of Africa to those of Asia. Ask your student, "What do they have in common?," "Which features are different?," and "How could these similarities and differences affect the stories of each continent?"

Answer Key

Explore

All the cities have a river or water source near them.

(Sidebar) Answers will vary. Possible answers: People might want to live near mountains. People might not want to live near swamps.

Write (Why are cities located near sources of water?)

Answers will vary. Possible answers: Cities are located near sources of water because they provide humans with food, water, and transportation. People can get fish and hunt other animals that live near the water. The soil near sources of water is usually more fertile to grow crops. They can get water from rivers and streams to drink. They can use a boat to easily get from one place to another.

Write (How are the mountains and steppes of Asia different?)

Answers will vary. Possible answers: Mountains are very tall, while steppes are flat grasslands. Mountains are often sources of rivers, while steppes provide food for livestock.

Practice

1. river delta
2. East Asia
3. North Asia
4. steppe
5. Mount Everest

Answers will vary. Possible answer: I am near the Indian and Pacific Oceans. I have a lot of islands, and many languages are spoken in my region. I am the (Southeast Asia) region.

Show What You Know

2. B, C, E, F, G

3. Answers will vary. Possible answers: People live near rivers because rivers provide people with two of their most basic needs—water and food. People live near river deltas because they provide fertile land that makes it easy to grow crops and provide easy access to good fish to eat. People live near mountains because they provide people with opportunities for hiking or skiing and greater access to wildlife. People who live near steppes are typically nomads and are following their livestock.

4. 1) E; 2) D; 3) C; 4) B; 5) F; 6) A

Lesson Objectives

By the end of this lesson, your student will be able to:

- examine evidence of common patterns and features of human settlements in Asia
- compare and contrast human settlements of Asia's different regions
- analyze how the environment influenced settlements in Asia

Supporting Your Student

Read

As your student reads about each region in Asia, ask them to compare and contrast the types of jobs and the way of life of the people living in the three different regions. You may ask, "How is the way that people make a living in the Himalayas similar to that of the people living in the Eastern Steppe?" or "How are the homes that people build on the Eastern Steppe different from those that are built in the river valleys?" This helps your student build connections between the different regions and the patterns of settlement between them.

Write *(List one way the settlements in the Himalayas are similar or different to those of the Eastern Steppe or the river valleys.)*

Help your student plan a response to the writing prompt by helping them to create a Venn diagram to organize their thoughts on how the settlements are the same or different. Reread the sections of text about those regions and have your student highlight similarities in one color and differences in another. Then, add the information to the Venn diagram in the correct areas. After that, have your student use the information to list a way the settlements are the same or different.

For example:

Himalayas   Eastern Steppe

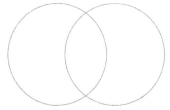

Practice

Help your student by first talking about the different environments present in each of the regions. Then, brainstorm ways that the environment might affect the people. Ask your student, "What would your life be like if you lived in the cold mountains of the Himalayas?" or "How do you think the lack of water in the Eastern Steppe affects the people who live there? What would they have to do in order to survive? Is this similar or different from the things the people in the river valley need to do to survive?" Encourage your student to go back to the text to find evidence of the effects of the environment on the people living there.

Learning Styles

Auditory learners may enjoy listening to stories of people who have climbed Mount Everest or of Mongols who live on the Eastern Steppe.

Visual learners may enjoy looking up additional pictures online of each of the places that were described. Your student could select two pictures of the same place and analyze the visual differences between the pictures, such as what landforms or man-made things are shown in each.

Kinesthetic learners may enjoy constructing a replica of a yurt and then describing the benefits of this type of housing for the nomads living on the Eastern Steppe.

Extension Activities

Home Connection

Discuss the environment around the place where you live. Talk about the different ways the environment affects the people living in your town, city, or state. Have your student draw a picture of what you discuss, such as drawing pictures of people's homes or the jobs that they do based on your area's environment.

Let's Play

Invite your student to pretend that they are a settler. Allow them to dress up and pretend to go scouting for a place to live. Join them in their pretend game. They should use ideas from the text to support why they are choosing to settle where they are and what they will do once they get there. They could also play through this activity with toys.

Answer Key

Explore

Answers may vary. Possible answers:

Picture 1

- People living near the ocean might fish for a living.
- The clothing that people wear in the area near the ocean would be light and breezy because it looks hot there.
- People in this area live in houses or apartments that are permanent.

Picture 2

- People living near the pasture might farm or raise animals.
- They would wear clothing that was tough and could get muddy from working on the farm or with the animals.
- The people living here might have more land and a home with a barn for their animals.

Write *(What caused people to settle in the river valleys?)*

Answers may vary. Possible answer: The river provided water for them to drink and grow crops.

Write *(List one way the settlements in the Himalayas are similar or different to those of the Eastern Steppe or the river valleys.)*

Answers will vary. Possible answers:

Differences:

- People living on the Eastern Steppe live in yurts and move from place to place while people living in the Himalayas may have more permanent homes.
- People living in the river valleys farm while people in the Himalayas are sherpas.

Similarities:

- People in river valleys and the Himalayas both live in small villages.
- All people raise livestock.

Practice

Region	Environment	Effect of Environment on People
Himalayas	Cold, high elevation Mountains	People have to build permanent shelters Use yaks Need to stay warm Become traders and mountaineers
Eastern Steppe	Cool, dry climate Cold in the winter Grassy areas	People have to move to find water and grass Need to stay warm Have to have easily movable shelters
River Valleys	Warm, moist climate Rivers	People can grow crops almost year round People become farmers Many people live here Cities can turn into huge metropolises Easy access to food and water Permanent homes are common

Show What You Know

1. A

2. B

3. True

4. Answers will vary. Possible answer: The common patterns of settlement between the regions in Asia include settling in a place where people have access to food and shelter. People also settle where they have access to water to drink.

5. Answers will vary. Possible answer: Yurts were used by people living on the Eastern Steppe because they needed homes that could be easily moved from one place to another. This is because they traveled with their livestock and did not have permanent homes.

6. Answers will vary. Possible answer: People in the Himalayas have adapted to their environment by using yaks to help them carry supplies in cold areas and by learning to be excellent mountain climbers.

7. Answers will vary. Possible answer:

Similarities:

- People living in the river valleys and mountains often live in permanent homes
- People on the Eastern Steppe and the Himalayas tend livestock
- The weather on the Eastern Steppe and in the Himalayas can be very cold

Differences:

- People in the river valleys and mountains have permanent homes while people on the Eastern Steppe often live in yurts which can be easily moved
- People in the Himalayas and the Eastern Steppe rely on livestock to help them move and trade while people in the river valleys are less dependent upon livestock
- People in the Himalayas use yaks to help them
- People in the Himalayas are often traders or sherpas

Lesson Objectives

By the end of this lesson, your student will be able to:

- identify features of the physical geography of Asia
- analyze the influence that people's relationship to natural resources had on the development of various Asian civilizations

Supporting Your Student

Read

As your student reads through the text, check in with them and ask them to describe the similarities and differences between the different civilizations. You should focus on the way the rivers helped to support large populations of people. Being able to support large populations led to the creation of larger cities and more powerful civilizations. The rivers allowed people to practice agriculture, which allowed them to stay in one place and develop permanent villages and cities. Over time, they built great structures that can still be seen today.

Write *(What are two similarities you can find between the Indus River Valley civilization and the Fertile Crescent civilization?)*

Help your student to make connections between the Indus River Valley and the Fertile Crescent civilizations. Ask them what the two places had in common. They should mention that the rivers flooded, which brought excellent soil to the area. They may also point out that both societies practiced agriculture.

Practice

Help your student find the sections in the text that talk about the different physical features. Help them identify where each physical feature is located based on what the text says. Then, prompt your student to identify why the physical feature is important. For example, you could say, "If someone is sick, why might it be important to be near the rainforest?" (Rainforests have plants that can be used to make medicine.)

Learning Styles

Auditory learners may enjoy hearing folk music from people living in the different areas of Asia mentioned in the lesson.

Visual learners may enjoy creating their own pictures of what they think each early civilization may have looked like.

Kinesthetic learners may enjoy pretending to be a river by acting out what it might look like to flood and deposit soil. They could also pretend to be farmers or the first settlers to a region and could pretend to be building the cities like the people they have read about.

Extension Activities

Civilization Research

Help your student perform extra research on one of the civilizations they read about. Ask them to keep a journal of their findings and to draw pictures of the different man-made and physical features in or around each civilization.

Science Connection

Find two seeds and two paper cups (or two other containers.) You will also need soil and a little bit of fertilizer. Fill both containers with soil and plant a seed in each container. Poke a hole in the bottom of the container for drainage. Put fertilizer in one container and not in the other. Water the fertilized container once every other day, and water the non-fertilized container once a week. The plant in the fertilized container should grow better than the other plant. Explain that the fertilizer represents the lush soil that is deposited by the Indus, Tigris, and Euphrates Rivers. Explain that the extra water in the cup represents the flooding of the rivers and why some of the plants receive more water than others. Ask your student what they notice about how the plant grows and what connections they could make to the text.

Answer Key

Explore

Answers may vary. Possible answers: People live near rivers so they can fish or travel more easily.

Write *(What are two similarities you can find between the Indus River Valley civilization and the Fertile Crescent civilization?)*

Answers may vary. Possible answers:

- The rivers in both places regularly flood and deposit lush soil and nutrients that help crops grow.
- Both of the civilizations are built on the banks of rivers.
- The rivers allow people to plant crops and build permanent settlements.
- Being farmers gave people more time to build monuments and cities.

Write *(Explain how the people in the Indus River Valley, Fertile Crescent, and China used soil and the rivers to develop their civilizations.)*

Answers may vary. Possible answers: The people living in the Fertile Crescent, the Indus River Valley, and China used the soil and the rivers to develop their civilization by using them to plant crops. These crops were able to feed large amounts of people, and their civilizations became powerful and large.

Practice

Answers may vary. Possible answers:

Rainforest: Plants provide food and medicine.

All rivers: Rivers provide water for drinking and for crops, make the soil more fertile, and provide a way to travel by boat.

Tibetan Plateau: Water flows over the rich soil and ends up on farms for Chinese farms to grow crops.

Himilayan Mountains: Snow from the mountains melts, which makes the rivers overflow and pick up soil from the plateau to deposit it on Chinese farms.

Show What You Know

1. Answers may vary. Possible answers:

Physical Feature	Sketch or Drawing	Important Characteristics
Rainforest	Drawing of trees, maybe some animals interspersed	80 inches of rain per year A lot of vegetation
Desert	Drawing of sand, maybe some dunes	Very dry Hard for people to live there
Mountain	Drawing of a mountain	Mountains provide snowmelt, which feeds rivers. They are tall and rocky
Plateau	Drawing of a large, tall, flat, mountain	Flat, arid The Tibetan Plateau is very cold and hard to live on
River	Drawing of a river with plants growing around it. There may be farms nearby	Fertile soil, access to water, sometimes flooding.

2. Answers may vary. Possible answer: The most important natural resource for the development of civilizations across Asia was rivers. Rivers led to the rise of most of the early civilizations in Asia because they allowed the people to practice agriculture and set up permanent settlements. This also gave them more time to build monuments and cities. The people of the Khmer empire were even able to build Angkor Wat with all of their extra free time. Another way that rivers helped civilizations across Asia to develop was by providing them with enough food to feed large populations of people. More people meant that the civilizations became more powerful. Obviously, rivers were the most important natural resource for the development of civilizations across Asia.

Lesson Objectives

By the end of this lesson, your student will be able to:

- explain ways that people in Asia made changes to their environment and how they responded to changes in the environment

Supporting Your Student

Read

While your student is reading all of the sections, ask them clarifying questions. You may ask, "Why do you think the people of the Indus River Valley civilization needed to move?" or "Do you think it was a good idea for China to build the Three Gorges Dam?" Be sure your student also understands the cause of the changes the people made to the environment or the reaction they had to the change. For example, ask "Why do the people of Tonle Sap Lake have to build their homes on stilts?"

Write (How have the people of Asia adapted to the changes in their environments?)

Before your student writes, help them analyze the Migration and Fish Farming sections, looking for ways that people have adapted to their changing environment. You may ask, "What happened to the Indus River? How did the people living near it respond? Why do you think they responded that way?" or "How did the people in Asia respond to the change in their rivers and oceans? How did they overcome the pollution that was reducing the number of fish that were available to them?"

Practice

For the practice portion, your student will need to decipher what problems the villagers are facing and which solutions from the text would be most effective in alleviating those problems. Encourage your student to underline or highlight the problems the villagers are facing. Then, have them either write down or tell you which solutions would be best to mitigate the problem. Have them refer to the Read sections for ideas that people in Asia have already used to adapt to or change their environment.

Learning Styles

Auditory learners may enjoy listening to a podcast that is focused on the Three Gorges Dam or aquaculture.

Visual learners may enjoy examining or drawing pictures that show the changes in the environment described in the lesson.

Kinesthetic learners may enjoy trying to build some of the solutions that were explained in the text, like the homes on stilts or the plant-covered buildings, out of household materials or craft supplies.

Extension Activities

Changes in Another Country

Do an internet search with your student on how people in the United States have overcome environmental changes or have changed their environment to suit their needs. One place to look at is Las Vegas, Nevada. You and your student could investigate how they bring enough water into the desert to support the city. This will most likely lead to an investigation of the Hoover Dam.

Closer Look

Work with your student to investigate how changes in climate can affect weather or the environment. Discuss different ways for people to overcome some of these changes. You and your student might come up with ways to mitigate forest fires or rising sea levels. The solutions don't have to be practically implemented as long as your student is thinking of ways that people could adapt to these environmental changes.

Answer Key

Explore

Answers will vary. Possible answers:

Rainforest

- Wide-brimmed hat
- Sunglasses
- T-shirts

Antarctica

- Winter coat
- Winter hat
- Gloves

Write *(How have the people of Asia adapted to the changes in their environments?)*

Answers will vary. Possible answer:

When the Indus River dried up or changed course, the people who were living near it migrated away. They needed to move to find a new river valley in which to settle. The people who live in Asia overcame the reduction of available fish by creating fish farms. This gave them more fish to eat and sell.

Practice

Answers will vary. Possible answers:

Problem	Solution
Flooding river	dam, stilt houses, migrating
Not using electricity to cool their homes	buildings covered in plants, buildings cooled by cold water pumped through pipes
Reduced fish in the river	fish farm, efforts to increase breeding of fish

Show What You Know

1.

Type of Problem	Flooding River	Warming Climate	Lack of Food
Solution	dam building stilt houses migration	covering buildings in plants pumping cold water through pipes in houses	fish farming migration

2. A. Dams
   B. migrating
   C. Adapting

3. Answers will vary. Possible answers:

- Explanation of dam building and how the dam helps to mitigate flooding
- Fish farming and an explanation on how fish farming helps to provide food when rivers are polluted or oceans are overfished
- Houses built on stilts to account for yearly flooding
- Cooling homes in a warming climate by covering them in plants or pumping cold water through pipes to cool them

Lesson Objectives

By the end of this lesson, your student will be able to:

• identify the physical processes that contribute to the availability and abundance of the natural resources found in Asia

• compare and contrast the availability and distribution of natural resources in Asia across regions

Supporting Your Student

Explore

As your student is getting ready to read, ask them what kinds of things they use in their everyday life. Ask them what they think the objects are made out of and if they think the objects are man-made or are made by nature. Discuss the idea that many of the things we use every day are found in nature or made from things in nature. Reiterate that resources found in nature are called natural resources and are found all over the world.

Read (Natural Resources in Asia)

As your student reads, they may need help understanding how coal and oil are formed. You may want to discuss the concept of intense heat and pressure with them. Ask your student, "What is pressure?" Have them demonstrate pressure by squeezing a grape or other type of fruit. Then ask, "How did the fruit change when you applied pressure to it?" Put the squashed fruit into the microwave in a microwave-safe dish. Microwave for 30 seconds. Ask your student, "How did the fruit change when you heated it up? What do you think would happen to the fruit if we applied pressure and heat for a very long time?" Connect the experiment to the lesson by explaining that when algae, plankton, and dead plant matter are subjected to heat and pressure for a very long time, they undergo changes just like the fruit did.

Write (List the conditions that must exist in order for coal and oil to be formed.)

Talk to your student about the conditions that must exist for oil and coal to be formed. Remind them of what the areas where these resources are found looked like many years ago (i.e., swamps, underwater).

Learning Styles

Auditory learners may enjoy creating and singing a song about the different natural resources they have discovered and where they are found in Asia.

Visual learners may enjoy drawing symbols to represent the different resources that they have read about on a map of Asia.

Kinesthetic learners may enjoy building a replica of a coal mine out of craft materials.

Extension Activities

Country Study Resource Map

Help your student create a resource map for their country study. Print out or sketch a blank map of your student's chosen country. Research the different natural resources found in the country. Help your student create symbols to represent each of the natural resources and then help them draw the symbols on the map where the different resources are found.

Closer to Home

Help your student research the natural resources found in your hometown or region. Ask your student how the natural resources affect the community and what life would be like if those resources did not exist.

Answer Key

Explore
Answers will vary. Possible answers: water, trees, animals, vegetables, fruits

Write *(List the conditions that must exist in order for coal and oil to be formed.)*
Answers will vary. Possible answers:

Oil: pressure, heat, plankton or algae, area that was once underwater

Coal: dead plant matter, area that was once a swamp

Practice

Country Name	Resource
Russia	coal, oil, forest
China	coal, water, fish
Myanmar	teak forest
Thailand	teak forest, fish
Indonesia	coal, teak forest
Saudi Arabia	oil
Iran	oil
Iraq	oil
United Arab Emirates	oil
Pakistan	water

The two countries with the widest variety of natural resources are China and Russia.

Show What You Know
1. A
2. B
3. A, D
4. B
5. C
6. B

LESSON 18
Natural Resources Lead to Trade

Lesson Objectives

By the end of this lesson, your student will be able to:

- identify key natural resources found in Asia
- describe how the use, distribution, and importance of natural resources can affect different groups in Asia
- identify the impact of trade on the availability of natural resources in Asia

Supporting Your Student

Read

While your student is reading or after they finish reading each section, ask them what the main idea of the section was and how it connects to the main idea of the previous section. Ask them to make connections to the world around them. For example, you might ask them, "What kinds of luxury goods are important in your life?" or "Can you think of any countries that have an abundance or scarcity of natural resources?" Discuss the consequences of having an abundance or scarcity of natural resources with your student.

These provide a great opportunity for comparing and contrasting. Help your student see how the availability of natural resources in China and Japan are similar and different by asking guiding questions, such as:

- Why was China able to trade their silk?
- Why is Japan able to trade their fish?
- How does Japan being an island affect its availability of resources compared to China?

Practice

Drawing a picture or creating a thinking map will help your student organize their thoughts for this story. They need to understand that both countries have problems. Their country needs oil while the other country needs rice. Discuss with your student how they would go about solving this problem. They should eventually reach the conclusion that they should trade with the other country. After they have decided this, ask them how the characters in their story would make this happen. When they have a

good idea of what they would do, ask them to write!

Learning Styles

Auditory learners may enjoy keeping an audio journal of the things they want and the things they need over the period of one to two days. Then they can indicate whether those wants and needs came from natural resources.

Visual learners may enjoy plotting out the Silk Road on a piece of paper or drawing pictures of the main idea of each section of reading.

Kinesthetic learners may enjoy pretending to go on a journey on the Silk Road. They could create the trade route through their neighborhood and pretend they are buying and selling goods, specifically silk from China and gold, silver, and wool from Europe.

Extension Activities

Let's Build!

Help your student build a replica of the Silk Road out of clay or play-dough. They can make each of the countries that the Silk Road went through out of a different color of clay and then build flags for those countries out of toothpicks and paper. When the map is finished, ask them to present it to someone else and explain the importance of the Silk Road to trade between Europe and Asia.

Natural Resources Podcast

Find a podcast that talks about the importance of trading natural resources between countries. This does not necessarily have to be between Asia and other countries, but that would be best. After listening to the podcast, ask your student to make connections between the podcast and what they read about in the lesson. How does scarcity and abundance of resources affect the countries mentioned in the podcast?

Answer Key

Explore

Answers may vary. Possible answer: If you lived in Russia and wanted teak wood, you could trade another type of wood to get teak wood in Russia.

Write *(What are some specific goods Asia produces that are sought by people all over the world? Why do you think people want these goods?)*

Answers may vary. Possible answer: Some goods Asia produces that are sought after are luxury goods like diamonds, gems, and delicious teas. People want these goods because they are rare, and owning rare items is considered a status symbol.

Write *(Why did Japan begin to trade?)*

Answers may vary. Possible answer: Japan began to trade because they did not have enough natural resources because they have little land. This is called scarcity. They do not have enough oil or coal, and so they trade for those resources to provide energy for their country.

Practice

Answers will vary. Your student should have discovered that both countries need something from the other country. They should write about trading their natural resource with the other country to get the natural resource they need.

Show What You Know

1. A, B, C, D
2. A
3. B
4. A
5. B
6. C

Lesson Objectives

By the end of this lesson, your student will be able to:

- identify the factors that led to the migration of people from a region in Asia
- describe the influences and contributions of the migrants to the new region in Asia

Supporting Your Student

Read

While your student is reading, ask them questions like "How would you feel if this happened in our hometown?," "Do you think we would migrate? If so, where would we go?," and "If not, how would we deal with the environmental change, natural disaster, new government, etc.?" Discuss the causes and effects of human migration to make sure your student understands why migration happens.

Read (Political Unrest)

During the communist revolution, people who did not agree with the new government were often put into jail or worse. People wanted to escape this punishment and the new regime, so they chose to leave. Explaining this to your student can help them better understand why people would have migrated away from China and Vietnam during the communist revolution.

Practice

In order to fill out the chart, your student will need to go back to the text to figure out what the characteristics of each reason for migration are. You should help your student generalize characteristics for each section. For example, people migrate due to environmental reasons because something happens that makes it impossible or difficult to live in their home region. This may be due to environmental change or natural disasters.

Learning Styles

Auditory learners may enjoy listening to podcasts or watching videos about people who have migrated from their home regions to settle somewhere else. First-person accounts will help your student understand this process from the point of view of someone who has gone through it.

Visual learners may enjoy creating a map that follows the route that migrants have taken. After reading the text, they could show the path that Muslims and Hindus took when migrating between Pakistan and India or the path that Chinese migrants took when escaping communism.

Kinesthetic learners may enjoy thinking about and packing items that they would carry with them if they were forced to migrate from their home. Challenge your student to only bring those things that are absolutely necessary.

Extension Activities

New Opportunities

Talk to your student about some jobs that they know of that used to exist and why they do not exist anymore. Some examples include panning for gold, telephone operators, or video store clerks. When you have discussed some different jobs that no longer exist, discuss which new jobs took their places. Reiterate that this happens all the time in our world, and talk about how it connects to the technology job boom that is taking place in India. Connect this to the lesson by emphasizing that many people in India are drawn to these higher-paying jobs and migrate from their homes to larger cities for these job opportunities.

Walk and Talk

Take a walk with your student. As you are walking, chat about the reasons for human migration. Talk to them about why people move. Ask if the student has ever moved. If they have, why did they move? If not, ask them what it might take for their family to decide to move. Ask if they know anyone who has moved from a different country or region, and discuss why their family might have made the decision to move.

Answer Key

Explore

Answers will vary. Possible answers: new jobs, to feel safe, their home was destroyed, they do not like the government

Practice

Migration Reasons	Characteristics
Environment	People need to migrate due to climate or environmental changes like flooding, droughts, or natural disasters, such as tsunamis and earthquakes.
Political Unrest	Change in government or the creation of a new country causes people who do not agree with the new government or do not feel like they fit into a new state to leave.
Development	Dams or railroads take up a lot of space. Human developments sometimes mean that people have to migrate to make room.
New Job Opportunities	Sometimes old ways of living are no longer needed, or technology takes the place of humans like in farming. Farmers move to the city for new jobs. Some people move to different cities that are known for certain types of jobs like tech jobs.

Write (How do migrants influence and contribute to their new regions?)

Answers will vary. Possible answers: Migrants bring new ideas, new cultural traditions, new types of food, and new religions.

Show What You Know

1. E
2. C
3. B
4. A
5. Answers will vary. Possible answer: When people migrate to a new region, they bring new ideas, food, religions, and cultural traditions with them.

Lesson Objectives

By the end of this lesson, your student will be able to:

- identify cultural features found in Asia
- describe how cultural features in a region of Asia influence factors of daily life, such as the economy, government, or transportation

Supporting Your Student

Read (Religions)

While your student reads about the religions of Asia, it may be helpful to pull out a physical map of Asia to have them better grasp where certain religions originated. For example, as your student reads about Islam, a religion that originated in the country of Saudi Arabia in West Asia, have your student point to this particular country and region on the map. Encourage your student to do the same with other Asian religions. Then, ask your student to think about the influences these locations had on the spread of religions throughout Asia. For example, if a trade route passed through a location, how did people in the region, such as Islamic merchants influence the spread of Islam?

Read (Transportation)

Help your student visualize the variety of transportation in Asia by using an online search engine to pull up images or video clips of unique vehicles, such as the rickshaws and tuk tuks of South Asia. These additional resources may assist your student to better understand why these vehicles are important and necessary in highly crowded streets. For example, rickshaws are small vehicles that have three seats and are very efficient in winding and curving around large groups of people in the congested streets of India.

Practice

Assist your student in completing the chart by asking them to refer back to the worktext as needed. Have your student fill in one column at a time to avoid confusion or rushing through this section. As your student reviews the worktext, have them highlight or write down bullet points of relevant information.

Encourage your student to list one or two examples from the worktext, such as "Hinduism can influence the economy because the Vedas teach people to engage in honest business practices."

Learning Styles

Auditory learners may enjoy listening to an audio file or podcast on different types of religion and art in Asia.

Visual learners may enjoy reading religious folklore such as the *Ramayana* and the *Mahabharata*, which are two of the most popular and widely-read books in India.

Kinesthetic learners may enjoy constructing models of small transportation vehicles, such as tuk tuks and rickshaws.

Extension Activities

Recreate Mughal Paintings!

Have your student investigate different Mughal paintings by using an online search engine. Then, ask your student to select one or two paintings of interest and recreate each painting using colored pencils or watercolor paints. You may wish to look into online videos or written tutorials on Mughal painting techniques. As your student recreates each painting, encourage them to think about the meaning and significance of each piece of art.

Country Study: Bulletin Board

Have your student select a country of interest in Asia and ask them to research three different cultural features in that country by using an online search engine. Then, ask your student to sketch the selected country on paper and attach it to a bulletin board. If your student does not have a bulletin board, a cutout of the country will work well. Encourage your student to pin or tape different cultural features to the country and add labels or captions to describe them. As your student creates their bulletin board, encourage them to think about how these cultural features have influenced the country's economy, government, or transportation.

Answer Key

Write *(Name three similarities and differences between Hinduism, Islam, and Taoism.)*
Answers may vary. Possible answers:

Similarities: Hinduism and Taoism are polytheistic religions, or the worship of many gods. Hinduism and Taoism believe in the idea of reincarnation.

Differences: Hinduism has a caste system, while Islam and Taoism do not. Hinduism originated from South Asia, Islam originated from West Asia, and Taoism originated from East Asia. Unlike Hinduism and Islam, Taoism started as a philosophy and later became a religion.

Write *(Name two unique features of the different types of art in Asia.)*
Answers may vary. Possible answers: Religions such as Hinduism and Taoism encourage people to be honest and fair when engaging in business; Islam has influenced the creation of an Islamic Republic, which uses strict rules from the Quran to govern people in society; countries with large populations have influenced the creation of many types of transportation, such as tuk tuks, and countries that have deserts have limited transportation because not many people live in these areas.

Practice
Answers may vary. Possible answers:

Transportation: High populations require more vehicles to transport people from region to region. Low populations in desert areas require fewer vehicles to transport people and make it hard for people to build roads.

Economy: Hinduism and Taoism encourage people to engage in honest and fair business practices so they can avoid punishment and prevent being reincarnated as undesired animals or insects.

Government: The Hindu caste system makes it hard for lower castes and the Dalits to get jobs in the government.

Show What You Know
1. A, B, D
2. Answers may vary. Possible answers: The shahada (to declare one's faith to God and the prophet Muhammed), the salat (to pray five times a day), the zakat (to give to those in need), the sawm (to fast, or stop eating and drinking), and the hajj (to make a pilgrimage to the holy city of Mecca at least once in a lifetime).
3. C
4. B
5. E

Lesson Objectives

By the end of this lesson, your student will be able to:

- investigate the cultural geography of Asia
- explore influences of Asian culture on individuals and civilizations around the world
- discover the lasting impact of Asian culture on everyday aspects of life

Supporting Your Student

Read (Food)

As your student reads about the types of food in Asia, it may be helpful to use an online search engine and look for additional images of coriander and cassia. This will help your student to visualize the shape, structure, size, and texture of these plants. Encourage your student to also look through images of popular ethnic dishes made with coriander, such as the Israeli falafel. They can also view images of dishes made from cassia, such as the cassia seed tea that is popular in China, Japan, and Korea. As your student looks through these images, ask them to think about how these cultural foods are grown, where they're grown, and how they have influenced people's way of life in Asia and around the world.

Read (Technology)

As your student reads about papermaking, printing, and flying machines, it may be helpful to find additional images and video clips of these historic achievements by using an online search engine. For example, to help your student better understand how the Chinese made paper, look for articles or video clips that discuss the process of making paper from mulberry trees. Encourage your student to compare the Chinese papermaking process to other ancient civilizations, such as the Egyptians, who used papyrus, and to modern-day papermaking processes. Ask them: "How are ancient and modern papermaking processes similar and different? What are the challenges and complexities of these methods?"

Practice

Assist your student in completing the bubble map by asking them to refer back to the worktext as needed.

Have your student fill in one bubble at a time to avoid confusion or rushing through this section. As your student reviews the worktext, have them highlight or write down bullet points of relevant information. For example, to complete the "Influences of Cultural Features in the World" section, encourage your student to list one or two examples from the worktext. Examples include: Early papermaking technology by the Chinese led to the invention of the Gutenberg printing press in Europe. Or, the flying machines developed by Firnas influenced the flying designs of Leonardo da Vinci and the flying machines of the Wright Brothers hundreds of years later.

Learning Styles

Auditory learners may enjoy listening to a recording or podcast about the types of foods in Asia, how to make them, or their influences around the world.

Visual learners may enjoy watching a documentary on how papermaking and printing by the early Chinese influenced the development of the Gutenberg printing press and modern printing systems.

Kinesthetic learners may enjoy creating models of Asian pagodas or stupas.

Extension Activities

Supermarket Scavenger Hunt

With your student, head to your local grocery store to search for popular Asian herbs and spices. For example, if your student was searching for coriander, have them look through the fresh produce section or in the dried herbs and spices aisle. While many Asian spices and herbs are sold in local markets, encourage your student to exercise patience, as not all items may be found. As your student completes the scavenger hunt and finds items, ask your student to describe the shape, size, color, and texture of each herb or spice.

Chinese Papermaking

Have your student recreate some of the steps used by the ancient Chinese to make paper. To do this, use an online search engine and ask your student to research articles on how to simulate the Chinese papermaking process. Modern-day materials for this activity will typically include newspapers, art paper or construction paper, water, small window screen, wood/frame, plastic tub, and blender. As your student creates their own paper, encourage them to think about the potential challenges of using bamboo and plant fibers, which were materials that the ancient Chinese used, to make paper.

Answer Key

Write (What are two cultural influences of the coriander and cassia plants?)

Answers may vary. Possible answers: Coriander is also used in traditional medicine to relieve stomach aches and boost the immune system. Cassia was an ingredient of anointing oil in Biblical times.

Write (How do Buddhist and Hindu temples differ in their architecture?)

Answers may vary. Possible answers: Hindu temples were usually dedicated to their different gods. Hindu temples were also frequently decorated with sculptures and carvings of different gods and goddesses along the exterior walls. Buddhist temples were dedicated to Buddha and did not have as many sculptures outside the temples.

Practice

Answers may vary. Possible answers:

Food: coriander and cassia

Architecture: pagodas and stupas

Technology: papermaking and flying machines

Show What You Know

1. Answers may vary. Possible answers: Coriander are small, round seeds that come from cilantro and are used to make popular dishes in West Asia, South Asia, and Southeast Asia. Cassia is a type of cinnamon that is often used in East Asian and South Asian food, such as teas, desserts, and meats; their influences include that coriander is used to flavor many dishes, including African couscous, Mexican guacamole and salads, and Italian pastas. Coriander is also used in traditional medicine to relieve stomach aches and boost the immune system. Cassia was an ingredient of anointing oil in Biblical times. Cassia is also used to flavor dark chocolates sold around the world.

2. C, B, E

3. A, B

4. B

5. Answers may vary. Possible answers: The flying inventions of Firnas influenced the flying designs of Leonardo da Vinci and the flying machines of the Wright Brothers. Today, airplane wings are designed from the knowledge of wind currents.

Lesson Objectives

In this lesson, your student will review the following big ideas from Chapter 2.

- The continent of Asia has diverse physical features, but most Asian cities with large populations are located near bodies of water and river deltas where resources such as fresh water and fertile soil can be found. (Lesson 13)
- Smaller wandering populations called nomads live on the steppes, or harsh grasslands. (Lesson 13)
- Countries with an abundance of natural resources, such as coal, oil, water, and forests, can use them for trade. (Lesson 17)
- A variety of resources on small islands like Japan are scarce, so Japan trades its abundant supply of fish for supplies it needs. (Lesson 18)
- Rare luxury resources, such as silk, brilliant diamonds and gems, and delicious teas, can help nations build wealth through trade. (Lesson 18)
- Migrants contribute to new communities when they move due to job opportunities, environmental changes, political unrest, or natural disasters. (Lesson 19)
- The importance of religion in Asian cultures can be seen in art, architecture, economy, and government. (Lesson 20)
- Asian spices, architecture, and invention have influenced the world. (Lesson 21)

Supporting Your Student

Create

Provide options to your student for this assignment. You can give your student the option of creating their design on a computer draw program or even using needle and thread to embroider a design on fabric. Encourage your student to review previous lessons, pictures, and worktext, to get ideas for their artwork.

Review (The Importance of Resources)

Encourage your student to review Chapter 13, "The Geography of Asia," specifically the section discussing the six regions of Asia. Remind your student that Russia is an extremely large country, but not all of it lies in Asia. The majority of Russia's population, along with its government, lies in Europe.

Practice (Asian Culture)

Encourage your student to use their worktext to find cultural features, but also to use their own experiences. Ask your student what they know about the religion, food, language, history, and governments of Asian countries. Perhaps they have experience with Asian music, television, or movies. Give your student the opportunity to add more circles to the graphic organizer to provide even more cultural features.

Learning Styles

Auditory learners may enjoy reading Asian folktales. Remind your student that these tales are cultural features too and that they can contain other cultural information.

Visual learners may enjoy conducting online research to find Asian art. Looking at art from different Asian countries can provide cultural information too.

Kinesthetic learners may enjoy researching and playing sports and games popular in Asian countries.

Extension Activities

Yangtze River Watercolor

Create a watercolor painting of the Yangtze River. Using watercolors for this art assignment provides the opportunity for your student to "flood" the banks of the river just like the water does in real life. Use photographs from online research or your worktext to give your student ideas for their piece of art.

Map of the Silk Road

Print a blank copy of a map of Asia. Have your student research and create a trade route map for the Silk Road. Discuss the fact that the Silk Road was not just one road but numerous roads and routes by land and sea to Europe and Africa. The Silk Road brought Asian cultures to other parts of the world and other world cultures to Asia.

Answer Key

Write *(How does trade help the nations of Asia?)*

Answers may vary. Possible answer: Trade allows nations to export abundant goods and import goods that are scarce.

Write *(How has Asian culture been shared globally?)*

Answers may vary. Possible answer: Trade has helped share Asian culture through the export of luxury goods such as silk. Ideas, religion, art, and architecture have also brought Asian culture around the world. Hinduism and Islam are popular religions outside of the United States. Pagodas and jewelry inspired by Asian religions are also appreciated around the world.

Practice *(Vocabulary)*

1. steppes
2. river delta
3. abundant
4. scarce
5. cultural feature
6. Luxury resources
7. migrate
8. communism
9. displaced

Practice *(Cause and Effect)*

Cause	Effect
China has an abundant supply of iron.	China exports iron to other nations.
Japan has a scarce supply of agricultural resources.	Japan imports many goods.
China found that other nations wanted luxury resources such as silk.	China exported these goods along the Silk Road.
Natural disasters such as earthquakes destroyed communities.	Populations migrate.
Human development projects such as dam building need land.	Populations are displaced.
Communism causes political unrest in China.	Many people move to other nations.
River deltas such as those next to the Yangtze River have plentiful resources.	Populations settle nearby.

Practice *(Asian Culture)*

Answers will vary. Possible answers: Chinese silk, spices, tea, communism, Hinduism, Buddhism, Islam, pagodas, jewelry

Quick Review

Refer to the statement your student circled in the Show What You Know section to self-assess their knowledge of the chapter concepts. Then to assist in determining if your student is ready to take the assessment, consider:

- Having your student explain how Asian countries make resources available to the people.
- Having your student explain what can cause a population to migrate.
- Having your student explain what they have learned about cultural features of Asia.

Chapter Assessment

1. Why did large populations first settle in Asia near river deltas?

   A. The river deltas flood each year.

   B. They wanted to live in the mountains.

   C. Freshwater and fertile soil were good for farming.

   D. Resources were scarce near the river.

2. The populations living on the steppes in Asia _____.

   A. were nomads

   B. created large cities and towns

   C. cut down timber to export

   D. had plentiful fresh water in the rainy climate

3. If a country has more than enough of a resource, the resource is _____.

   A. imported

   B. thrown away

   C. wasted

   D. exported

4. Name three natural resources found in Asia.

   ....

   ....

   ....

5. What resource is abundant in Japan? How does Japan use this resource?

   ....

   ....

   ....

6. What is the Silk Road? Describe how this "road" influenced trade.

   ....

   ....

   ....

7. If a person is displaced, they _____.

   A. were forced to relocate or move from their home

   B. decided to move to a new place for a job

   C. want to learn a new language

   D. want to live near family and friends

8. Hinduism, Buddhism, and Islam are _____.

   A. political systems in Asia

   B. Asian languages

   C. religions which originated in Asia

   D. types of artwork appreciated around the world

9. What are cultural features? Describe a specific cultural feature of Asia.

....

....

....

10. True or False   In China, a shift to communism caused political unrest and migration.

Chapter Assessment Answer Key

1. C

2. A

3. D

4. Answers will vary. Possible answers: coal, iron, timber, fish, petroleum, water

5. Answers will vary. Possible answers: Fish is an abundant resource in Japan. They use fish to trade for scarce resources.

6. Answers will vary. Possible answers: The Silk Road was a series of trade routes used to trade silk, spices, and other goods throughout Asia, Africa, and Europe. It increased trade and brought Asian culture to other parts of the world.

7. A

8. C

9. Answers will vary. Possible answers: Cultural features are aspects of culture or a way of life. Religion, language, food, and art are all cultural features. Religions such as Hinduism, Buddhism, and Islam are cultural features. Hinduism is a polytheistic religion, so there are multiple gods. These gods are often pictured in art, jewelry, or symbolized in architecture.

10. True

Alternative Assessment

Project: Letter of Advice

Project Requirements or Steps:

Your friend has decided to migrate to Asia. You decide to write them a letter telling them all that you know about the land, resources, and culture. Use vocabulary from this chapter and important facts and details that show your mastery of the content.

1. Add the date to the top of your letter. Then begin your letter with a greeting.

2. Ask your friend why they have decided to migrate to Asia. Tell your friend what you know about other individuals or populations who decide to migrate to new places. What effect can migrants have on their new homes?

3. Tell your friend about the geographical features of Asia. What place should they visit? Are there any areas your friend should avoid? Be sure to explain why you feel the way you do.

4. Where do you think your friend should live while they are in Asia? What types of resources are available there and why are they available?

5. What can you teach your friend about the cultural features of Asia or the specific place you recommend living in Asia?

6. Wish your friend luck with their adventure and provide a closing and signature at the end of your letter.

60

Discover! SOCIAL STUDIES • GRADE 5 • CHAPTER 2 ASSESSMENT

Alternative Assessment Rubric

Use the following rubric to grade your student's assessment.

	4	3	2	1	Points
Geography	The letter includes several details regarding geographical features of Asia and shows knowledge of countries and regions in Asia.	The letter includes details regarding multiple geographical features of Asia as well as knowledge of specific countries or regions in Asia.	The letter includes details regarding at least two geographical features of Asia.	The letter includes details regarding one geographical feature of Asia.	
Migration	The letter provides several details regarding the cause and effects of migration.	The letter includes at least two reasons populations migrate and discusses at least one effect of migration.	The letter includes at least one reason populations migrate.	The letter shows understanding of the term *migration* or *migrate.*	
Resources	The letter describes several natural resources as well as the effects of trade when resources are abundant and scarce.	The letter describes multiple natural resources as well as the effects of trade.	The letter describes multiple natural resources found in Asia.	The letter describes a resource one finds in Asia.	
Cultural Features	The letter describes several cultural features and their global influence.	The letter describes multiple cultural features and how these have influenced the world.	The letter describes two cultural features of Asia.	The letter describes a cultural feature of Asia.	

Total Points _____/16

Average _____

Discover! SOCIAL STUDIES • GRADE 5 • CHAPTER 2 ASSESSMENT

61

Lesson Objectives

By the end of this lesson, your student will be able to:

- examine different maps of Central America
- determine the story a map of Central America can tell
- compare and contrast the location of cities and geographic features in Central America and your community

Supporting Your Student

Online Connection
Guide your student to find maps of the area you live in. Help them to identify the geographic features of your area and important parts of your community.

Explore
Help your student name information that the maps tell you. For example, help your student identify locations of specific places, where to visit, how to get from point A to point B, and information about the physical environment of an area.

Read (Geopolitical and Tourist Maps)
Remind your student of the three types of maps they learned about (topographic, geopolitical, and tourist). Students may struggle with identifying the stories these maps tell. Help guide them to think about what each map tells them under the Read section.

Read (Cities in Central America)
Guide your student to help them identify the map and pictures present. Discuss with them their community and what may be similar and what is different from the maps and pictures of Central America. Your student may struggle coming up with similarities and differences with their community and these images. Help them to identify similarities, such as mountains, volcanoes, and forests.

Learning Styles

Auditory learners may enjoy asking others to explain the similarities and differences observed on various maps. They may also want to share the similarities and differences between where they live and the maps of Central America through a podcast.

Visual learners may enjoy creating an online slideshow or poster to identify the different types of maps they have learned about. They can also draw maps or pictures or create collages of their community.

Kinesthetic learners may enjoy going out and exploring the geographical features in their community to compare and contrast to the geographic features in Central America.

Extension Activities

Create a Map
Choose a map: topographic map, geopolitical map, or tourist map. Have your student create a map of your home or community. Your student can do a digital drawing or notebook/poster drawing. They will identify geographical features, important parts of the community, and use their map to tell the story of the community that they live in.

Creating Map Stories
Have your student choose a map of either the community they live in or a place they are interested in traveling to. Have your student write a story about the map. For example, they can pretend to be a traveler wanting to visit a certain area of the country. Your student would choose a tourist map and create this story based on the map. They can plan where they would go based on the map and describe their plan for their travels. Another example would be looking at a topographic map and seeing which landforms your student student can identify. They can write a story about the elevation of the land and what type of elevation this country has. Your student can write or type their story.

Answer Key

Write *(How do tourist maps help tourists?)*
Answers will vary. Possible answers: These maps show destinations that are important in a city. These maps show information on how to get to different parts of the city.

Practice
Answers will vary. Similarities are: Guatemala City, Guatemala, San Salvador, El Salvador, and San Jose, Costa Rica are all cities located in Central America. They are all largely populated, near volcanoes, and prone to earthquakes. Differences are: They are located in different countries; Some are capital cities; San Jose used to be a capital city.

Show What You Know
1. B
2. A
3. A
4. C

Examining Geographic Features in Central America

Lesson Objectives

By the end of this lesson, your student will be able to:

- analyze geographic factors that influence where people live in Central America
- identify the significance of key physical geographic features in Central America
- compare and contrast patterns of human settlements of different regions in Central America
- analyze how the environment influenced these settlements

Supporting Your Student

In the Real World

For this activity, encourage your student to think about the things in the community they like to do. Does your student like to go for walks, go swimming or fishing, etc.? What features help them do this activity? Help prompt your student with some fun things your family does in the area you live.

Explore

Discuss each picture with your student. Help them identify what the picture is showing. The first image is a waterfall in a rainforest. The second picture is a volcano near a body of water. The third image is bananas being farmed. Try to have your student identify what kind of places would have these three distinct features. Discuss with them what they have in common. For example, bananas grow in warm areas, and rainforests are warm areas. Discuss what your student's geographic area is like. Do they have any features in common with these pictures, or do they live in a completely different environment?

Read (Geographic Features of Central America)

What are some geographic similarities and differences that jump out to you between your location and Central America? Your student may have trouble coming up with similarities and differences, so guide them. A difference may be the lack of volcanoes where you live or no mountains. A similarity could be proximity to the coast. Point out different geographic features in your area and in the different regions of

Central America. Allow them to identify if they are similar or different to Central America.

Write (Choose a region that you think would be the best area to live in. Provide at least two reasons why you chose this area.)

Your student may struggle coming up with ideas of why people might want to live in the coastal region as opposed to further inland when looking at the map. Remind your student what they read about humid weather in these countries. If you have ever been to the ocean or a lake or river, talk about what the air feels like there. Discuss how that feels different than when you first get out of the shower and the air in the bathroom is all hot and sticky. Which type of air would be better to live in? Guiding them should help them make connections.

Learning Styles

Auditory learners may enjoy listening to the sounds of the rainforest in Central America.

Visual learners may enjoy drawing pictures of the geographic features present in Central America.

Kinesthetic learners may enjoy going on a walk and identifying various geographic features in your area.

Extension Activities

Create a Map

Consider having your student make a physical map of the geographic features in Central America. Have them draw the features and also identify the different populations in each country. See if your student can identify if the geographic features play a role in where people live.

Central America Commercial

Consider having your student create a commercial for Central America explaining the information they have learned from the lesson. Allow them to write a script encouraging someone to visit Central America. They should provide information about Central America's geographic features, its population, and its agriculture.

Answer Key

Explore

Answers will vary. Your student should point out that the pictures show waterfalls, mountains, and bananas growing in a tropical region. These pictures all show beautiful areas with lots of green plants growing.

Write *(Choose a region that you think would be the best area to live in. Provide at least two reasons why you chose this area.)*

Answers may vary. Possible answer: I want to live in the Atlantic lowlands because they have tropical rainforests. I want to live in the Central Highlands because they have volcanoes. I want to live in the Pacific lowlands because this is where a lot of people live.

Practice

Answers will vary. Possible answers:

Central Highlands: short, dry season; moderate amounts of rain; mountains; pine tree forests; 40 volcanoes, many islands

Both: human settlement more popular here; heavily populated; agriculture strong

Pacific Lowlands: narrow plains; borders the Pacific Ocean; extended dry season; high temperatures

Show What You Know

1. B
2. False
3. A, C
4. C
5. Answers will vary. Possible answer: The tropical climate caused people to live in less humid areas where crops are grown. These areas are also great for agriculture because of the fertile soil from old volcanoes. People live closer to the areas with the volcanoes since they do allow for agriculture.

LESSON 25
Physical Geography of Central America

Lesson Objectives

By the end of this lesson, your student will be able to:

- describe the physical geography of Central America
- analyze the influence of people's relationship to natural resources in Central America

Supporting Your Student

Explore
Your student may struggle coming up with information about what humans need to survive. Remind them that water, food, and shelter are needs. For example, having transportation is a want and not a need. Guide them to see that everything we have is made from Earth's resources. Some may be easy to find outside in your backyard, while others you will need to buy at a store because they can only be found in other countries or areas.

Write (How have people affected natural resources in Central America?)
Your student may struggle coming up with how people have affected natural resources. Have them look back to the previous reading section. Reread the preceding paragraph carefully and support them with this reading. Help them understand that when there is a limited amount of resources, they could run out. For example, if there are a limited number of fish and they are caught instead of being allowed to reproduce, it will be hard to replenish the fish population.

Practice
Your student may need help identifying what natural resources are used for. In the first image, help them see that the trees can be used for lumber. Lumber can be used for anything that contains wood, like paper, desks, and houses. For the water, discuss that all living organisms need water to survive. The last image is a banana tree. Discuss with your student if they have ever eaten bananas and how often. They will realize this is a natural resource used for food and the buying and selling of bananas contributes to the country's economy.

Learning Styles

Auditory learners may enjoy listening to songs from Central America. You can go online and research "Central American Songs" or "Songs Native to Central America." Your student may also create their own song about Central America that discusses its physical geography.

Visual learners may enjoy looking at various images of different physical features in Central America. You can go online and research "Physical Features of Central America."

Kinesthetic learners may enjoy going outside and identifying natural resources they see on a walk, hike, or in the yard.

Extension Activities

Create a Brochure
Consider having your student make a physical map of the geographic features in Central America. Have them draw the features and also identify the different populations in each country. See if your student can identify if the geographic features play a role in where people live.

Scavenger Hunt
Consider having your student go on a physical features scavenger hunt. List two or three physical features in your community and have your student search for them. This can be small scale and using resources just around the instruction site or can be done on a larger scale, using a car.

Answer Key

In the Real World *(Human-Made Vs. Natural)*

Answers will vary. Possible answers:

Human-Made Things: buildings, cars, phones

Natural Things: trees, rivers, flowers

Write *(How have people affected natural resources in Central America?)*

Answers will vary. Possible answers: The many natural resources have taken a toll on the Central American and Caribbean people and land. Due to its natural resources being unique, they are often needed throughout the world. This has resulted in over-mining and has caused loss of land for many people, animal species, and plant species. Many people native to Central America and the Caribbean Islands are asking for a change to help protect their countries and their natural resources.

Practice

	The physical feature shown is a rainforest. A natural resource in this image is lumber.	Lumber can be used for houses, paper, or any substance that uses wood.
	The physical feature is a waterfall. A natural resource is water.	All living things need water to drink.
	The physical feature is a rainforest, and mountains are in the background. The natural resource is food or bananas.	Bananas are used all over the world to eat.

Show What You Know

1. Any useful substance that can be found in nature, like water, forests, and fossil fuels

2. iron, copper, coffee, sugar, silver, rubber, lumber

3. economy

4. A

5. C

6. B

Changes in the Central American and Caribbean Environment

Lesson Objectives

By the end of this lesson, your student will be able to:

- identify how people make changes to and respond to changes in their environment
- describe the significance of the Panama Canal and the amazing capabilities of those who envisioned and built it
- examine ways people in Central America made changes to their environment
- illustrate examples of how they responded to changes in the environment

Supporting Your Student

Read

Your student may struggle with pronouncing some of the terms in the reading passages. For example, *deforestation* and *urbanization* may be challenging words. Guide them through the reading and help them see how many of the human-made changes to the environment often benefit people but damage the environment. For example, deforestation allows for more space to create human activities and needs, but takes away homes of plants and animals.

Write *(Think about the Panama Canal and its many successes. Write three ways this positively impacted the world. Use the text to support your answer.)*

Your student may have trouble with choosing three ways the Panama Canal positively impacted the world. Help guide them to go back into the text and look for their answers. Guide them to think about how that would improve their lives by allowing more trade and aid in job creation.

Practice

Your student will be successful in identifying the definition, but may have trouble drawing a picture. Your student may look at an image from the text or online to demonstrate a better image to create their own drawing. Your student may have trouble coming up with impacts on the environment. Help remind them to go back into the text and look through the examples provided.

Learning Styles

Auditory learners may enjoy listening to a podcast on environmental changes.

Visual learners may enjoy watching a video of a ship being lowered into the Panama Canal and gliding across the canal.

Kinesthetic learners may enjoy a game of charades to act out the different changes to the environment.

Extension Activities

In Your Own Backyard

Your student will choose one type of man-made change to the environment discussed in this lesson. Your student will research this change and identify it in their community. For example, maybe they are from near a coal mining town. They can research about how having a mine near them impacted their community.

Canal Ad

Your student will create an ad for another Panama Canal. They will advertise the positives of the current Panama Canal and ask for help building another canal. They must include the negatives of the job mentioned in this lesson!

Changes in the Central American and Caribbean Environment

Answer Key

Write *(Think about the Panama Canal and its many successes. Write three ways this positively impacted the world. Use the text to support your answer.)*
Answers will vary. Possible answers:

1. It connects the Pacific Ocean to the Atlantic Ocean.
2. It shortened trade routes.
3. It positively impacts the environment by creating faster routes for ships and cuts down on their waste of resources.

Practice

The Enviromental Change	Why the Change Took Place	Impact on the Enviroment
Agriculture is the practice of farming.	To grow crops for people to sell	Can take over land that was once for plants or animals
Deforestation is the cutting down of large groups of trees or forests.	To clear land for houses	Causes animals and plants to lose their habitat
Urbanization is the process of making an area into a city.	To make room for more people to move to cities	Takes the land from plants and animals Produce the air we breathe and take in the carbon dioxide we produce
Dam building is building a structure to hold back water.	To produce electricity To store water	Damages ecosystems in the water or on the shore
Mining is the process of digging to retrieve valuable resources.	To retrieve precious metals like gold or copper to sell	Digs underground, which can interfere with the land

Show What You Know

1. agriculture, deforestation, urbanization, dam building, and mining
2. False
3. Answers will vary. Possible answers: improvement in economy, found new places to live, move to more cities (urbanization)
4. Answers will vary. Possible answers: The Panama Canal impacted the world by allowing easier access for ships going to the Atlantic and Pacific Oceans and making trade easier across the world.

Lesson Objectives

By the end of this lesson, your student will be able to:

- identify the physical processes that contribute to the availability and abundance of natural resources
- compare and contrast the availability and distribution of natural resources in Central America

Supporting Your Student

Read (Physical Processes)

Your student may not remember what ways plate tectonics developed in Central America and the Caribbean. Your student may need to reread this section again and use the text to identify these answers. Have your student highlight or underline the areas in the text to help them see what plate tectonics created.

Read (How Physical Processes Affect Natural Resources)

Your student may struggle with some of the words found in this section. *Foresters*, *manganese*, and *cobalt* will most likely be unfamiliar to them. Stop and discuss with them what these words mean. If needed, have your student highlight unknown words throughout the passages to stop and discuss with you or use a dictionary or online tool to identify the definitions.

Practice

Your student may have a hard time identifying the differences in natural resources found in Central America and the Caribbean. Both of these locations are very similar and have many similar resources. Help them look for the differences to fill out the Venn diagram. Discuss with your student why these areas might have similar natural resources. They are both close to the equator, and they both have a lot of sun and many beaches, mountains, and volcanoes. Discuss that this closeness in geography and similarities in landscape make it more likely that they will have similar resources.

Online Connection

Your student will be looking for natural resources found in their community. Your student may struggle to identify the correct information to type into the search engine. Help guide them with the correct information and correct spelling of their community. For example, instead of typing in your town name, start with a broader topic like a province or state.

Learning Styles

Auditory learners may enjoy listening to the process of a volcano developing read aloud to them.

Visual learners may enjoy watching videos on volcanic formations or eruptions and taking a virtual tour of a limestone cave.

Kinesthetic learners may enjoy building their own volcano to erupt.

Extension Activities

Compare and Contrast Booklet

Have your student create a foldable booklet to compare and contrast two countries, for example, one country in Central America and one in the Caribbean Islands. They should use a search engine to research the physical processes that take place in these countries and research the natural resources. Then, have them fold a piece of paper in half two times. Then, unfold the paper. Draw a picture of one country on one half of the paper and draw a picture of the other country on the other side. They should cut the paper down the middle to create flaps to write underneath. Your student can color the foldable as well.

Natural Resource Commercial

Your student will research one natural resource found in Central America or the Caribbean Islands. They will create a commercial for this resource to "sell" it. They should write a script and perform this commercial to be successful in selling their natural resource. For example, they can choose bananas and write a commercial telling the audience everything they can do with bananas and why they need them.

Answer Key

Practice

Answers will vary. Possible answer:

Central America: lead, ore, natural gas

Caribbean Islands: cobalt, maganese, bauxite

Both: gold, silver, copper, oil nickel, timber, fish

There are more similarities than differences in natural resources in these two regions. This is due to their similar location to the equator, they are both surrounded by ocean water, and are both hot, humid climates.

Show What You Know

1. False

2. A, D

3. Answers will vary. Possible answer: Some natural resources in Central America and the Caribbean are gold, silver, oil, timber, limestone, fish, clay, glass, and steel.

4. Answers will vary. Possible answer: The natural resources in the Caribbean and Central America are similar because they are in very similar parts of the world. They are both surrounded by water, in tropical climates, and near the equator. Many of their natural resources, including fish, precious metals, and minerals, are similar because of their climate.

Lesson Objectives

By the end of this lesson, your student will be able to:

- identify key natural resources found in Central America
- describe how the use, distribution, and importance of natural resources can affect different groups
- identify the impact of trade on the availability of natural resources
- examine the significance of ecotourism in Costa Rica

Supporting Your Student

Explore

Your student will have to identify the last three food items they ate for the Explore question. If they are unable to do so, have them list three of their favorite foods instead. Discuss where these foods came from and how they got to your student.

Write *(Explain three differences in Haiti and the Dominican Republic.)*

Your student may struggle to understand why two places in such close proximity have such different poverty rates and availability of resources. Discuss with them that even though they are close in geography, they have experienced a very different history and treatment from other countries. Haiti has been treated poorly by governing countries and was unable to set up a successful government, while the Dominican Republic was treated well and was successful in creating its government. Haiti also has experienced more deforestation and therefore more issues with climate change, while the Dominican Republic has experienced far less deforestation.

Learning Styles

Auditory learners may enjoy discussing the differences in distribution of natural resources with family members.

Visual learners may enjoy looking at pictures of Costa Rica and seeing why it is important to keep tourism eco-friendly.

Kinesthetic learners may enjoy searching for natural resources around town. Take your student on a walk or on a car ride and point out the natural resources around them.

Extension Activities

Share Your Views With the United Nations

Have your student write a speech as if they are a person in the United Nations. Have them share with other members of the United Nations why different countries need to have better access to resources and why. Have them discuss why you believe people should have more equal access to resources.

Ecotourism Brochure

Have your student research a location they would love to visit in Central America or the Caribbean. Have them create a brochure for an ecotourism trip to this country. Encourage them to inspire others to take this ecotourism trip with them!

Answer Key

Write *(Explain three differences in Haiti and the Dominican Republic.)*

1. Haiti was not treated well by France. The Dominican Republic was treated better by Spain.

2. Haiti has experienced a lot of deforestation. The Dominican Republic has not experienced this much deforestation.

3. Haiti does not receive much rainfall for its crops. The Dominican Republic receives more rainfall.

Show What You Know

1. A, B, C, D

2. False

3. Answers will vary. Possible answer: Trade impacts Central America and the Caribbean by helping the economy and allows for people to share natural resources with other parts of the world. Some countries have many natural resources, but not a large population or money and have to export most of their products. Other countries have few natural resources and must import all of their products. This can cause unequal distribution of natural resources.

4. Ecotourism

Lesson Objectives

By the end of this lesson, your student will be able to:

- research the global impact of the Columbian Exchange on the distribution of people and resources across Central America
- describe the reasons that humans migrate
- identify the factors that led to the migration of people from one region in Central America
- examine the influences and contributions of the migrants to the new region

Supporting Your Student

Explore

Your student may struggle being able to answer the questions in this section. Help guide them by providing sample answers about your own family or friends or, if possible, by asking guided questions about their family. Your student may need to ask an adult in their family to be able to identify where their family originated from. If possible, allow them to use the computer to look at a more detailed map.

Write *(List one positive result and one negative result of the Columbian Exchange in Central America and the Caribbean.)*

To assist your student with the Write section, have them go back and highlight positives and negatives of the Columbian Exchange. This will help them answer the questions much more easily.

Practice

To help your student with the practice, have them reread the section aloud to make sure they are comprehending it. Discuss with your student why these reasons are important and what each one means. Your student may need a refresher on what *economic* and *political* mean. Discuss with them that *economics* refer to how goods are bought and sold in a country and that *politics* are how a country is governed.

Learning Styles

Auditory learners may enjoy recording themselves reading the following sections: "The Columbian Exchange", "Migration Reasons", and "Migration in Central America" and listen back to the recording.

Visual learners may enjoy watching a video explaining the Columbian Exchange.

Kinesthetic learners may enjoy acting out the process of migrating and planning what they would bring if they were to migrate to another area.

Extension Activities

Columbian Exchange

Have your student research information about the Columbian Exchange for their country. They will identify how this exchange impacted the country they are from. Have them write about the different plants, animals, diseases, and more introduced by the Columbian Exchange.

Dream Location

Have your student create a dream location to migrate to. Have them plan what to pack, who to bring, and why they are choosing to go to this place. For example, it could be a location with great jobs for everyone and plenty of safety. Have your student create a poster for this place and try to persuade other people to join them.

Answer Key

Write *(List one positive result and one negative result of the Columbian Exchange in Central America and the Caribbean.)*

Answers will vary. Possible answers: A positive of the Columbian Exchange was having more animals to help in the fields, which improved the economy. A negative was the spread of diseases from other areas that killed many people.

Practice

Reasons	Example	Picture
Economic	Migrating to a new place for a job	Pictures will vary.
Political	Migrating to a new place because you disagree with the politics	Pictures will vary.
Safety	Migrating to a new place because it is unsafe where you live	Pictures will vary.
Environmental	Migrating because your home was harmed by flooding	Pictures will vary.
Social	Migrating to a new place because your family lives elsewhere	Pictures will vary.

Show What You Know

1. C
2. False
3. C
4. Answers will vary. Possible answers: People are migrating from some Central American countries because they are not able to find jobs, these countries are not safe for their families, or their homes are being harmed by environmental reasons like flooding.

Lesson Objectives

By the end of this lesson, your student will be able to:

- identify the location of key cultural features in Central America and the Caribbean
- relate how cultural features in a region of Central America and the Caribbean influence population, the economy, government, and transportation

Supporting Your Student

Read (Art, Language, and Religion)

As your student reads the features and influences of art, language, and religion in Central America and the Caribbean, it may be helpful to have a physical map of both regions available to help your student visualize where these locations are in the world. For example, as your student reads about the locations of the ancient Mayan civilization, point out where the Mayans would have been located in present-day Central America, Southern Mexico, and the countries of Central America. As your student reads about the ancient Taíno civilization and the areas they inhabited, present-day countries such as Puerto Rico and the Dominican Republic can also be pointed out on the map.

Write (How do improvements in technology and medicine influence the population and economy of Central America and the Caribbean?)

Help your student generate a response to this question by asking them to think about how technology and medicine may be relevant to their own life. Perhaps your student has gotten an X-ray or seen many tools at the dentist's office during a cleaning. Encourage your students to think about the importance of these medical tools and how they influence society. For example, X-rays detect broken bones and help people receive the treatment that they need, which improves their overall quality of life (population influence). However, X-ray machines are costly to make and expensive for people who need to get one (economic influence).

Learning Styles

Auditory learners may enjoy listening to recordings of endangered languages such as the Mayan language or extinct languages such as Taíno to hear the differences in pronunciation, tone, and sentence structure.

Visual learners may enjoy watching a video on how religions of the Mayans and Taíno were different. Your student may be especially interested in seeing the different forms of the gods that were worshipped by the Mayans and Taínos.

Kinesthetic learners may enjoy making models or replicas of famous Central American and Caribbean art such as the gold frog pendant of Central America and the pendant mask of the Taínos. These replicas could be made from common household items, including metals, jewelry, or clay. As your student builds these models or replicas, discuss the representation and influence of these art pieces in the regions that produced them.

Extension Activities

Write in Mayan Hieroglyphics

The Mayans developed a sophisticated written language using picture symbols known as hieroglyphics. With your student, research common Mayan hieroglyphics and examine what each symbol means. Encourage your student to practice drawing these symbols to create a fun message in the Mayan language! To learn more about ancient writing systems, your student may also wish to look into how Mayan hieroglyphics differ from other ancient writing systems, such as the hieroglyphics used by the Egyptians or the cuneiform devised by the Mesopotamians.

Cultural Features of Central America and the Caribbean

Create a Travel Itinerary

With your student, create a hypothetical travel itinerary from your residence to a country in Central America and a country in the Caribbean. Research the types of transportation that are available in these two countries, their respective costs, and how they influence the way of life of people living in those regions. Encourage your student to compare and present the findings by creating a presentation or brochure.

Answer Key

Write *(What examples of art, languages, and religions can be found in Central America and the Caribbean?)*

Answers may vary. Possible answers: The Mayans (Central America) used hieroglyphics in their art and written language and spoke the Maya language. The Taíno (the Caribbean) used petroglyphs as art and had no written language. The Taíno people spoke the language Taíno. Both civilizations worshiped many gods.

Write *(How do improvements in technology and medicine affect the population and economy of Central America and the Caribbean?)*

Answers may vary. Possible answers: Better technology has allowed for the creation of vaccines and medicines. Advances in technology have allowed societies to build more schools and increase job opportunities.

Write *(How do cultural features affect the creation of governments and transportation in Central America and the Caribbean?)*

Answers may vary. Possible answers: People's right to vote has influenced the creation of the presidential system. Lack of money to build main roads has created a smaller vehicle called the tuk tuk.

Show What You Know

1. A
2. C
3. Answers may vary. Possible answers: worshiping of many gods, using art to depict religion
4. Answers may vary. Possible answer:

Regions	Features That Influence Population	Features That Influence the Economy	Features That Influence the Government	Features That Influence Transportation
Central America and the Caribbean	technology, medicine	technology, medicine	shared beliefs (right to vote)	lack of main roads, economic hardships

Central American Culture and Its Influence

Lesson Objectives

By the end of this lesson, your student will be able to:

- investigate the cultural geography of Central America
- explore influences of Central American culture on individuals and civilizations around the world
- discover the lasting impact of Central American culture on everyday aspects of life

Supporting Your Student

Read (Musical Instruments)
Using an online search engine, find audio or video recordings of the cabasa and marimba instruments to help your student connect with the lesson. Encourage your student to investigate how these instruments are played by examining the structure, sound, and pitch of these instruments. As your student engages in the lesson, encourage them to think about the influences these instruments may have had among people on a local and global level.

Read (Science and Technology)
As your student reads through this section of text, it may be helpful to investigate the functions and uses of Mayan calendars, the Tzolk'in and the Haab', by using an online search engine. Discuss with your student the purpose of the decorated wheels that the Mayans used to indicate time and predict future events, such as moon cycles, eclipses, and the end of the world. Encourage your student to compare and contrast the differences of these calendars with the Gregorian calendar that is commonly used today.

Write (How did science and technology influence societies in Central America and the world?)
Assist your student in generating a response by relating some of these achievements, such as the Gregorian calendar, to their personal life. Encourage your student to think about the following questions: What might happen if calendars did not exist? How might that affect the way people live?

Learning Styles

Auditory learners may enjoy listening to recordings of different percussion instruments popular in Central America, such as the cabasa and marimba.

Visual learners may enjoy watching a video on the cultural features of the Mayan civilization, including religion, architecture, and food.

Kinesthetic learners may create models of ancient Mayan pyramids, such as Tikal, Tazumal, and Copán.

Extension Activities

Create a Central American Dish
With your student, create a popular Central American dish such as tamales, empanadas, or enchiladas. Help your student research and gather the ingredients used to make these foods. Discuss with your student the influences these dishes have had on many regions of the world. Encourage your student to compare these dishes to his or her favorite dish!

Musical History
Assist your student in making a visual timeline that tells the story of one or more Central American musical instruments. Help your student complete research online tracing the origins, influences, and modern uses of one or more of the instruments of their choice.

Answer Key

Write *(What instruments are played in Central America, and what were their influences in the world?)*

Answers may vary. Possible answer: Popular instruments in Central America include the cabasa and marimba. They influenced the creation of popular musical genres, such as the samba and bossa nova in Brazil, and reggaeton in Puerto Rico.

Write *(How did science and technology influence societies in Central America and the world?)*

Answers may vary. Possible answers: The number zero helped the Mayans measure time, distance, and space, and it is used all over the world today for the same reasons. The Mayans created calendars like the Tzolk'in for religious ceremonies and a solar calendar called the Haab' to track time. The Haab' was a 365-day calendar and is like the Gregorian calendar that we use today. Instruments like the loom helped the Mayans weave clothing and create paints like glitter. Glitter is used around the world today to decorate items.

Write *(How did food influence societies in Central America and the world?)*

Answers may vary. Possible answer: Corn, rice, beans, chili peppers, and tomatoes have influenced the creation of many famous Central American dishes, such as tamales, enchiladas, and empanadas, which are all made from corn dough.

Practice

Answers may vary. The following is an example of possible answers:

Cultural Features from Your Own Life:

1. Religion (Christianity, Judaism, Islam, etc.)
2. Language (English, Spanish, French, etc.)
3. Music (an instrument that your student plays or listens to)

Influences on Daily Life:

1. going to church on a regular basis
2. reading and writing in English, Spanish, and French; can easily communicate with people from different regions of the world such as Europe, Central America, North America, and South America
3. practicing the piano often to compete in music festivals and competitions

Show What You Know

1. C, E, F
2. B
3. Answers may vary. Possible answer: The Mayan invention of the number zero is used to measure time, distance, and space. The Mayan invention of looms has helped many to weave clothes.
4. C

Lesson Objectives

By the end of this lesson, your student will review the following big ideas from Chapter 3.

- Different maps can tell you different stories—topographic maps show the physical features of land, geopolitical maps tell a continent's boundaries and different countries within the continent, tourist maps help tourists navigate an unfamiliar city, and political maps show countries and cities. (Lesson 23)
- Geographic factors such as climate and vegetation, and geographic features such as volcanoes, the Pacific Ocean, the Caribbean Sea, rivers, and mountain ranges influence where people live in Central America. (Lesson 24)
- Natural resources influence people's relationship to the land in Central America and the Caribbean. For example, people make money by mining but they can also overmine and lose valuable natural resources. (Lesson 25)
- People make changes and respond to changes in their environment through agriculture, deforestation, urbanization, dam building, and mining. (Lesson 26)
- Volcanoes, earthquakes, and erosion contribute to the availability and abundance of natural resources like gold, silver, fish, and forests. (Lesson 27)
- Gold, copper, and fish are key natural resources found in Central America. (Lesson 28)
- The Columbian Exchange impacted the distribution of people and resources across Central America. (Lesson 29)
- Key cultural features of Central America and the Caribbean include art, language, religion, shared beliefs, and technology. (Lesson 30)
- Cultural features like architecture, music, science, technology, and food in Central America have influenced civilizations around the world. (Lesson 31)

Supporting Your Student

Practice *(Visualizing Vocabulary)*
Help your student visualize important vocabulary by encouraging them to think of an image that is best associated with the word. To do this, it would be helpful to have your student look through images that are associated with the word. For example, when defining the word culture, your student may think of a favorite food (e.g., pizza) or a favorite architecture (e.g. Egyptian pyramids). Encourage your student to draw basic features of both to reinforce the idea that culture encompasses more than one characteristic.

Practice *(Identifying and Understanding Cultural Features)*
Help your student complete the table by identifying two cultural features in Central America and the Caribbean. Encourage your student to refer to the corresponding chapter lessons to investigate which region(s) in Central America and the Caribbean these key cultural resources were found or derived from, their uses, and their influence in the world. For example, thousands of indigenous languages were spoken in the Americas before the arrival of the Europeans. They are now either extinct or endangered, because major languages of Central America, like Spanish, Portuguese, and English, and the Caribbean, like Spanish, English, and French Creole, have replaced older languages.

Practice *(Compare and Contrast)*
Your student may struggle with finding similarities or differences between the geographic or cultural features of Central America and the Caribbean. It will be helpful for your student to look at the graphic organizers they filled out on the previous page. For example, if your student listed art as a cultural feature in Central America and the Caribbean, encourage your student to look for any noticeable patterns. This could be what the art depicts. In fact, Central American and Caribbean art expressed very similar themes such as religion and natural disasters.

Learning Styles

Auditory learners may enjoy listening to a podcast on the geographic and cultural features of Central America or the Caribbean.

Visual learners may enjoy taking a virtual or in-person trip to a natural history museum or art gallery to learn more about the geographic and cultural features of Central America or the Caribbean.

Kinesthetic learners may enjoy creating their own documentary to highlight the geographic and cultural features of Central America or the Caribbean.

Extension Activities

Virtual or In-Person Field Trip

Choose two regions in Central America or the Caribbean to explore with your student and take a virtual or in-person field trip. Watch videos, explore photographs, and participate in simulations and field excavations. As your student explores each region, have them keep a journal of their virtual field trip, such as taking notes on the location, climate, physical features, and cultural features.

Role-Play: What's That Region?

Have your student create a drawing of a region in Central America or the Caribbean and provide two or three clues about the region without giving you its name. Then, guess the region's name. You may wish to take turns while completing the activity.

Answer Key

Practice *(Visualizing Vocabulary)*
Check your student's definitions and drawings to make sure they relate to one another.

Practice *(Identifying and Understanding Cultural Features)*
Answers will vary. Possible answers:

Type of Cultural Feature: Art (Hieroglyphics)		
Location	Use	Influence in Central America and the World
Central America	to depict natural disasters; religious beliefs; can be used as a written language	communication between peoples; influenced the writing system of succeeding civilizations such as the Aztecs; creation of present-day holidays (Día de Los Muertos - Mexico)

Type of Cultural Feature: Art (Petroglyphs)		
Location	Use	Influence in Caribbean and the World
The Caribbean (present-day Puerto Rico and the Dominican Republic)	to depict religion, astronomy, and way of life of the Taíno	religious representation to honor to the gods and goddesses; discovery of the Taíno civilization by examining petroglyphs left in rock caves

Practice *(Compare and Contrast)*
Answers will vary based on whether your student chooses to compare and contrast cultural or geographic features. Refer to the Support Your Student section to see an example of an acceptable answer.

Quick Review

Refer to the statement your student circled in the Show What You Know section to self-assess their knowledge of the chapter concepts. Then to assist in determining if your student is ready to take the assessment, consider:

- Having your student look at different maps of Central America and the Caribbean to identify the types of maps they are (i.e., topographic vs. geopolitical). Discuss with your student the unique characteristics of each map that is viewed.

- Having your student create a Venn diagram to compare the geographic or cultural features of Central America and the Caribbean that they learned from this chapter. Discuss with your student the similarities and differences of the chosen features in both geographic regions.

Chapter Assessment

Fill in the blanks using the vocabulary words in the Word Bank below.

Word Bank: cultural feature   topographic map   geopolitical map
geographic features   Columbian Exchange   natural resources

1. Art is an example of a _____.

2. Known as the _____, this process transferred plants, animals, culture, human populations, technology, diseases, and ideas among the Americas, Europe, Asia, and Africa.

3. Gold, copper, and fish are examples of the types of _____ you would find in Central America and the Caribbean.

4. Volcanoes, mountains, and coastlines are examples of a region's _____.

5. A _____ highlights the physical features of the region.

6. A _____ defines the borders of the region's countries and cities.

Chapter Assessment Answer Key

1. cultural feature
2. Columbian Exchange
3. natural resources
4. geographic features
5. topographic map
6. geopolitical map

Alternative Assessment

Project: Infographic

Project Requirements or Steps:

You will create an infographic to show features of different regions in the world. An infographic is a chart or diagram used to convey information or data quickly and clearly. Use the following steps to create your infographic.

1. Select at least two regions you studied in the chapter. Gather information about the features of these regions.

2. Create a title for your infographic related to the topic.

3. Include photos and drawings related to the topic.

4. Include information or data to explain and support the photos and drawings you included.

5. Include at least two similarities between the features of the regions you selected.

6. Present the information in a creative way.

Discover! SOCIAL STUDIES • GRADE 5 • CHAPTER 3 ASSESSMENT

85

Alternative Assessment Rubric

Use the following rubric to grade your student's assessment.

	4	3	2	1	Points
Connection to the Chapter	The infographic is clearly connected to the chapter.	The infographic is connected to the chapter.	The infographic is somewhat connected to the chapter.	The infographic is not connected to the chapter.	
Creativity	The infographic is very creative and aesthetically appealing.	The infographic is creative and aesthetically appealing.	The infographic is somewhat creative and aesthetically appealing.	The infographic is not creative or aesthetically appealing.	
Information	The information or data is accurate and easy to follow.	The information or data is accurate.	The information or data is somewhat accurate.	The information or data is not accurate.	
Grammar and Mechanics	There are no grammar and punctuation mistakes.	There are one or two grammar and punctuation mistakes.	There are several grammar and punctuation mistakes.	There are a distracting number of grammar and punctuation mistakes.	

Total Points _____/16

Average _____

86

Discover! SOCIAL STUDIES • GRADE 5 • CHAPTER 3 ASSESSMENT

Lesson Objectives

By the end of this lesson, your student will be able to:

- examine different maps of Europe
- determine a story a map can tell about Europe
- compare and contrast the major cities in Europe and the cities in your state or country

Supporting Your Student

Explore

If your student is having trouble coming up with their own ideas, they may benefit from hearing your ideas first. Consider finding a picture on the map and giving a short sentence about that picture as a starting point. For example, you might point out the guitar shown in Spain and ask your student to think about why the guitar might be shown on the map (because that type of music is popular in Spain). Help your student see that the landmarks, foods, clothing, and other items displayed all tell about the unique or important characteristics of each country and their culture or way of life.

Write (Compare this map to the geopolitical map of Europe that you looked at. What is one thing that is the same about the maps? What is one thing that is different about the maps?)

If your student struggles with this activity, draw attention to the shapes that each border makes. How did these shapes change between the two maps? Have your student trace the border of a modern-day European country with their finger and then trace the same area on the older map to feel the difference in how the borders change. Additionally, point out how the labels that tell the name of a certain country or area may or may not have changed. In some areas, like Sweden, the name may have stayed relatively similar, but the borders of the country could be different.

Read (Cities in Europe)

This section is meant to spark further curiosity about cities throughout Europe. As your student reads about each city, ask them to talk about a similarity or difference from the previous city. This will help them when they get to the Show What You Know section.

Practice

Assist your student in locating information about their own city or town. You could look at maps, brochures, and complete online research about your town or city. As your student investigates their own city or town, look for opportunities to compare and contrast their findings with a European city. For example, you may point out how your city has a lot of churches just like Rome, Italy.

Learning Styles

Auditory learners may enjoy listening to national anthems from different countries in Europe. Have them search for a country's national anthem by using a search engine and typing "national anthem of _____." Ask your student if any words seem especially important as they listen to several different national anthems.

Visual learners may enjoy drawing their own map of Europe. They may also enjoy drawing a picture of themselves at a certain age and then drawing another picture of themselves at different age. For example, students may decide to draw a picture of themselves as a baby and then later as a 10-year-old. Draw attention to the fact that things change over time, which also happens with maps of places.

Kinesthetic learners may enjoy acting as a compass to travel to different countries in Europe. Have them take steps forward to act out the northern direction. Have them take steps backward to act out the southern direction. Have them take steps to the right to act out the eastern direction. Have them take steps left to act out the western direction. Have students use their body motions to explain what direction they are traveling to reach a different country in Europe.

Extension Activities

Play a Game: Guess Who I Am

Play a game of "Guess Who I Am" with your student. Decide who will be player one and player two. Player one chooses a country, tourist destination, or city in Europe. They should not tell player two their choice. Player one names various characteristics of their chosen country, tourist destination, or city within Europe that has been studied in this lesson. Player two tries to guess the destination with as few hints as possible. Then, switch roles.

Create a Travel Brochure

Your student can create a trifold travel brochure. The brochure should include a cover with an original title, relevant pictures, and your student's name. On the inside of the brochure, your student should describe three different countries and include two or three facts about each one. They should also draw the shape of each country according to the maps provided.

Answer Key

Explore

Answers will vary. Possible answers: In the map, you can see stories about people who are proud of their countries (there are a lot of people holding flags), stories of holiday celebrations, and stories about different types of buildings.

Write (*Many of the major cities on the map are located on or near bodies of water. Why do you think many cities are located there?*)

Answer will vary. Possible answer: Many cities are located near the water so people could travel, fish, or trade.

Write (*What is something you can learn about France from this map? What is a story that the map is telling?*)

Answer will vary. Possible answer: You can learn about the food, animals, and landmarks that are important to the people of France. There are pictures of a lot of boats around, which means people in France may like to sail. There are a lot of landmarks,

like a big tower (Eiffel Tower) and windmills, which can mean that a tourist would have a lot of sites to visit.

Write (*Compare this map to the geopolitical map of Europe that you looked at. What is one thing that is the same about the maps? What is one thing that is different about the maps?*)

Answers will vary. Possible answers:

Same: The continent is still divided into separate areas. Some of the names are similar like Ireland and Sweden.

Different: Some countries on the older map are not present on the current map, like the Kingdom of Leon and Castile. Other countries are bigger or smaller in size, like the Kingdom of France is smaller than modern-day France.

Practice

Answers will vary depending on the student's town or city.

Show What You Know

1. The first map should be circled.

2. True

3. Answers will vary. Possible answers:
   The first map is a topographical map. It is telling a story about the landforms in Europe. You can learn where mountains, plains, rivers, and oceans are in Europe from this map.
   The second map is a geopolitical map. It can tell you the story of wars that have been fought, as well as who won and who lost. You can learn the boundaries of the countries of Europe from this map.
   The third map is a tourist map. It can tell the story of the nationality of each country. You can learn the national flag of each country in Europe from this tourist map.

4. Answers will vary. Possible answers: I chose to compare Paris and London. They are similar because both were around in the time of the Romans. They are different because they speak different languages. Paris speaks French and London speaks English.

5. Answers will vary depending on the student's town or city. It should include information from the chart provided when discussing the European city.

Characteristics
• London is the capital of England.
• Its history stretches back to the times of the Romans.
• Major attractions include Big Ben, the Houses of Parliament, the Tower of London, and Westminster Abbey.
• Over 300 languages are spoken in London today.
• St. Petersburg was founded in 1703 by Peter the Great.
• It is located next to the Baltic Sea.
• It has been renamed three times.
• Berlin is the capital of Germany.
• Its history dates back to the 13th century.
• It has about 175 museums.
• Rome is the capital of Italy.
• It was founded in 753 BC.
• It is the most populated city in Italy with almost 3 million residents.
• It has 250 fountains and 900 churches.
• Paris is the capital of France.
• It was founded in 259 BC.
• Paris was originally a Roman city called "Lutetia."

Disc●ver! SOCIAL STUDIES • GRADE 5 • LESSON 33

89

LESSON 34
Geographic Features of Europe

Lesson Objectives

By the end of this lesson, your student will be able to:

- analyze geographic factors that influence where people live in Europe
- identify geographic features of Europe
- identify geographic connections between the continents

Supporting Your Student

Read

As you read this section, consider having your student sketch out what they think each geographic feature looks like that is not pictured in the text. Then, work with your student to look up what the feature actually looks like to confirm their hypothesis and allow them to make corrections.

Write (Pick one of the geographic features below. Write one advantage and one disadvantage of living in that location.)

To help your student think about the advantages and disadvantages of living near each geographic feature, ask your student to think of their own experiences with geographic features. Why would they want to live near the mountains? Why might they not want to live there? Have your student make a list of things they could do near each geographic feature. For example, they could hike or ski if they lived near the mountains. If they lived near the channel, they could fish, swim, or take a boat ride. Then have your student identify what might make it challenging to live near these locations. Guide them by asking questions about each feature, such as "What if you lived on a mountainside in the Alps and it snowed a lot? Would you still be able to travel into town to get what you need?"

Practice

Help your student with this section by pointing out various oceans. Ask your student which continents touch that ocean. Pretend you want to travel from one continent to the next. Ask your student how you would get there. Have them trace their path and see what geographic features they encounter. Are there geographic features that you would need to travel across to reach another continent?

Country Study

Continue the Country Study for Europe by helping your student find a map of the country. Help your student point out different geographic features on the map. Encourage them to see if any of the geographic features in this lesson are present in their country.

Learning Styles

Auditory learners may enjoy listening to the soundscapes present near various geographic features throughout Europe. For example, use a search engine to look up "sounds of the Alps."

Visual learners may enjoy drawing a map and labeling various geographic features on the continent of Europe.

Kinesthetic learners may enjoy acting out motions with their bodies that they would use at different geographic features throughout Europe. For example, tell your student that they are now at the Ural Mountains. Your student can act as if they are skiing or climbing up a mountain. This could also be done as a game of charades, where you or your student acts out different geographic features and guesses which one is being acted out.

Extension Activities

Geographic Feature Art

Your student can choose a geographic feature in Europe that they have studied. They can research pictures of that geographic feature in Europe and draw a picture of their favorite geographic feature. Be sure to label the specific name of the geographic feature in Europe and the country in Europe in which it is located.

Multimedia Presentation

Your student can create a multimedia presentation where they choose five different geographic features. Have your student define what each geographic feature is. Have your student include an image of each geographic feature in Europe and at least two locations in Europe where each geographic feature can be found.

Answer Key

Write *(Pick two of the geographic features on this page. What is one way they are similar? What is one way they are different?)*

Answers will vary. Possible answers: (Same) Plateaus and marshes are both found on land. (Different) Plateaus are flat pieces of land that may or may not have a lot of water, while marshes are land that is covered by water for long periods of time.

Write *(Pick one of the geographic features below. Write one advantage and one disadvantage of living in that location.)*

Answers will vary. Possible answers:

	Advantages of living near this geographic feature in Europe	Disadvantages of living near this geographic feature in Europe
Alps Mountain Range	• People exercise and are more active • Fresher air • Winter sports • Enjoy snow • More peaceful • Fewer people	• Usually further away from cities • Can be isolating; not as many people • Internet speeds can be slower • Harsh weather conditions
Tabernas Desert	• Sun is a good source of vitamin D • More peaceful • Fewer people • Better air quality	• Nights can be very cold • Days can be very hot • Infrequent rainfall • Harder for plants and animals to live • Further away from cities

English Channel	• Easy to travel to another country • Access to water sports such as fishing or surfing • Relaxing views	• Environmental risks such as oil spills • Tide changing can be dangerous • Salt can negatively impact homes

Answer Key

Practice

Answers will vary. Possible answers:

Geographic Feature	Continents Connected
Mediterranean Sea	Connects Europe to Africa
Pacific Ocean	Connects Australia to South America
Southern Ocean	Connects Africa to Antarctica
	Connects Australia to Antarctica
Indian Ocean	Connects Africa to Australia

Show What You Know

1. Answers may vary. Possible answers: plains, mountains, marshes, channels, canals, deserts, seas, oceans, lakes, rivers, foothills, plateaus

2. Answers may vary. Possible answers: plains, seas, mountains, rivers

3. Answers will vary. Possible answers: People may live by a water feature like a lake. They could fish in the lake, go swimming, or ride a boat. People might live by the mountains if they like to go hiking or skiing. People might live by a desert if they like drier weather.

4. D

5. B

Lesson Objectives

By the end of this lesson, your student will be able to:

- compare and contrast human settlements of different regions in Europe
- analyze how the environment influenced settlements in Europe

Supporting Your Student

Explore
To help your student answer the question, encourage them to think about the things that they like to do. This will help them notice features of the images.

Read (Mountain Settlements)
As your student reads this section in the worktext, it may be helpful to retrieve a physical map of Europe from an online search engine for your student to better visualize the distinct regions in Europe. For example, as your student reads about the Alps, which stretch from France in Western Europe to Slovenia in Eastern Europe, have your student locate the two countries on the map. Then, ask your student to follow the curvature of the Alps with their fingers on the map.

Learning Styles

Auditory learners may enjoy listening to a podcast about human settlements in European mountains, coastal cities, or lowlands.

Visual learners may enjoy watching a video about how the environment influenced European settlements, such as how the famous eruption of Mount Vesuvius changed the way of life in volcanic regions for farmers.

Kinesthetic learners may enjoy building models that depict specific European settlements.

Extension Activities

Human Settlement Flash Cards
Ask your student to create flash cards of different types of human settlements that they have learned about in Europe, including those on the mountains, plains, and coasts. Encourage your student to draw images and write down basic facts about the features of each settlement. For example, your student can draw mountains and vineyards to depict Italy. Have them include information such as the fact that people in these regions typically live in houses called chalets. This information can be written to highlight the residential features. To ensure that your student has ample space for drawing and writing, have them use flashcards with dimensions of five inches by eight inches or larger.

Connections to Home
Discuss the environment of your hometown with your student. Ask your student how the environment in which they live influences the way that people have settled. What kinds of homes are built? What kinds of jobs do people do that are dependent upon the environment? Have your student write their ideas down.

Answer Key

Explore
Answers will vary. Possible answer: The settlements in Croatia and Italy are both near water. The one in the Alps is not. I would like to live on the coastline of Procida, Italy because I love boats.

Write *(What are the advantages and disadvantages of mountain settlements?)*
Answers will vary. Possible answers: Advantages include soil that is rich in nutrients and good for growing crops, such as grapes to make wine. A disadvantage is that it is hard for people to access medicine and technology. There is also potential for dangerous volcanic eruptions.

Write *(What are the advantages and disadvantages of coastal settlements?)*
Answers will vary. Possible answers: Advantages include easy access to resources and a comfortable, temperate climate. Disadvantages include extreme weather such as hurricanes that can cause coastal erosion.

Write *(What are the advantages and disadvantages of settlements in the plains?)*
Answers will vary. Possible answers: The temperate climate is favorable for growing crops, such as wheat, rye, and barley all year round. Disadvantages include long periods of rain, which cause rivers to overflow and lead to flooding.

Show What You Know
1. Answers will vary. Possible answers:

   Settlement in the mountains—Alps, which stretch from France in western Europe to Slovenia in Eastern Europe

   Settlement in the plains—northwest Europe, such as Germany, France, Ireland, and Scotland, and eastern Europe, such as Ukraine and Russia

   Coastal settlements—popular coastal cities such as Porto in Portugal, Copenhagen in Denmark, Nice in France, Mykonos in Greece, Dubrovnik in Croatia, and Podgorica in Montenegro

2. A, B, D
3. B, C, D
4. C

Physical Geography and Natural Resources of Europe

Lesson Objectives

By the end of this lesson, your student will be able to:

- identify features of the physical geography of Europe
- analyze the influence of people's relationship to natural resources and its effects on the development of various European civilizations

Supporting Your Student

Read (Mountains)

As your student reads about the different mountain ranges in Europe, it may be helpful to have your student watch online video clips so they can see these mountains in 3D. For example, as your student reads about the Alps and the Carpathians, your student can point out unique features, including textures, sizes, shapes, heights, climates, animals, and vegetation in these areas. Encourage your student to compare the different features of both mountain ranges and discuss how these features influence the development of civilizations.

Read (Natural Resources and Early Civilizations)

As your student reads about the natural resources of Europe and how they have influenced the development of early civilizations, it may be helpful to use an online search engine to look through images of iron weapons made by the Celts, such as swords, shields, and javelins. Encourage your student to describe the features of ancient Celtic weapons and how they compare to the weapons that are used in modern society. Then, discuss how natural resources such as iron influenced the development of the Celtic civilization, followed by the Roman civilization.

Learning Styles

Auditory learners may enjoy listening to an audio recording of major European physical features, such as mountains, oceans, seas, and rivers, and then discuss how they influence climate.

Visual learners may enjoy watching a documentary on the importance of European physical features in the development of early civilizations, such as the Celts and Romans.

Kinesthetic learners may enjoy creating models of early European civilizations, such as the Celts and Romans, and feature important natural resources that were used.

Extension Activities

Create a Painting

Have your student create a painting of European physical features, such as the Alps, the Mediterranean Sea, or the Rhine River. Encourage your student to include details of a particular region, such as climate, animals, vegetation, and people. For example, if your student draws the Mediterranean Sea, encourage them to include cliffs, lush green vegetation in the mountains or on land, boats, clear blue waters, and colorful houses. As your student paints, ask them to think about how climate has influenced the environment and development of early civilizations along the Mediterranean Sea.

Answer Key

Write *(What are the differences between temperate and subtropical climates?)*
Answers will vary. Possible answers: Temperate climates have cool to warm summers and mild winters. Most of Europe has a temperate climate. Subtropical climates have hot, dry summers and cool, wet winters.

Write *(What oceans and seas define the borders of Europe?)*
Answers will vary. Possible answers: Europe is bordered by the Arctic Ocean to the north; the Atlantic Ocean to the west; and the Mediterranean, Black, and Caspian Seas to the south.

Write *(What were the influences of natural resources on the Celtic and Roman civilizations?)*
Answers will vary. Possible answers: Celts used iron to create advanced weapons. Romans used travertine in temples, monuments, and amphitheaters such as the Colosseum.

Show What You Know
1. A, D
2. temperate
3. A, B, C, E, F
4. B
5. A

Humans' Environmental Impacts in Europe (Part 1)

Lesson Objectives

By the end of this lesson, your student will be able to:

- identify ways that people in Europe have made changes to their environment
- identify examples of how people in Europe responded to changes in the environment
- describe the effects of land use conversion from forests to farmland and the depletion of Britain's forests due to World War I

Supporting Your Student

Read (Air and Water Pollution, Environmental Laws)

As your student reads through these sections in the worktext, it may be helpful to use an online search engine to pull up images or video clips that describe the causes and effects of air and water pollution. For example, when your student reads about nitrates, have them investigate why they are used in agriculture and how they disturb or kill plants and animals in the water by removing oxygen. It may also be helpful for your student to research regions in Europe that are greatly affected by air pollution, such as Naples in Italy and Paris in France, and areas that are affected by water pollution, such as the Danube and Sarno Rivers. Encourage your student to investigate why these cities and rivers in Europe are heavily polluted and if the Clean Air Package and Nitrates Directive have helped reduce pollution in these areas.

Read (World War I and the Environment)

As your student reads this section in the worktext, it may be helpful to use an online search engine to retrieve forest maps that show the large impacts of deforestation and reforestation. Specifically, assist your student in the research of available forests before, during, and after World War I in Europe. For example, before World War I, people in England excessively cut down trees to build and heat homes, make furniture, and construct ships. During World War I, the increase in demand for timber worsened deforestation so much that only about three percent of land was covered in forests. After World War I, reforestation efforts in England led to an increase in Britain's forests by about 10 to 12 percent as of 2010.

Practice

Help your student complete the table in the practice section by asking them to review the worktext and write down or highlight important points from each section. Ask your student to focus on one environmental feature at a time, such as air pollution, and how people have caused and responded to it. For example, factories and vehicle exhaust release nitrogen dioxide and carbon dioxide into the atmosphere, which can create smog and acid rain. Smog and acid rain can lead to global warming, which harms the environment. People have responded to the release of toxic gases by creating the Clean Air Package, which limits the amount of nitrogen dioxide and carbon dioxide in the air from factories.

Learning Styles

Auditory learners may enjoy listening to a podcast on World War I and how it influenced people and the environment.

Visual learners may enjoy watching a documentary of the impacts of air and water pollution in Europe.

Kinesthetic learners may enjoy creating an advertisement by discussing the harmful effects of water pollution on animals, insects, plants, and humans.

Extension Activities

What Are Air Pollutants?

Have your student research different types of air pollutants, such as nitrogen dioxide, carbon monoxide, sulfur dioxide, or ozone, and their sources by using an online search engine. Encourage your student to investigate how these air pollutants affect the environment, including people, plants, and animals in Europe and around the world. Have your student share their findings by creating a brochure or poster.

Construct a Water Pollution Model

Have your student research the different ways that people can contribute to water pollution, such as agricultural nitrates, oil spills, ocean littering, and radioactive wastes, by using an online search engine. Then ask your student to build a model showing all types of water pollution and describe how they can impact the environment. To encourage additional research, ask your student to investigate environmental laws that address water pollution in Europe and around the world.

Answer Key

Explore

Answers will vary. Possible answer: The government can create rules and regulations to stop people from littering, to keep water clean, and to encourage people to drive less.

Write (What kinds of human activities have caused air and water pollution?)

Answers may vary. Possible answers: Air pollution is caused by high levels of toxic gases, such as nitrogen dioxide and carbon monoxide, which are released from factories or the exhaust of vehicles. It is also caused by the release of carbon dioxide when fossil fuels are burned. Air pollution can harm all sorts of vegetation. Air pollution can also cause acid rain, which can kill fish in lakes and rivers. Water pollution can be caused by agricultural wastes like nitrates. Nitrates get created naturally when nitrogen, a nutrient for plants, is not fully used by plants that can get into water. High amounts of nitrates can harm or kill aquatic plants, insects, and animals. They can also be harmful to people's health.

Write (How did the Clean Air Package and Nitrates Directive affect the environment?)

Answers may vary. Possible answers: The Clean Air Package limits the amount of nitrogen dioxide that can be released into the air from factories. The Nitrates Directive monitors surface waters that have high amounts of nitrates and limits the amount of nitrogen that can be used by farmers to fertilize crops.

Write (How did World War I impact European forests?)

Answers may vary. Possible answers: Deforestation in England was so severe that by the end of World War I, only about three percent of Britain's forests remained. After World War I, people passed laws to protect European forests and made the cutting down of trees illegal in some areas.

Practice

Answers may vary. Possible answer:

Environmental Features	Features of Human Changes to the Environment	Features of Human Responses to the Environment
Air Pollution	nitrogen dioxide, carbon monoxide, methane from factories and vehicle exhausts; smog; acid rain; destruction of plant and animal habitats	Clean Air Package limiting the amount of nitrogen dioxide that can be released into the air
Water Pollution	nitrates reduce oxygen in rivers, lakes, and streams; harms aquatic plants, insects, and animals; pollutes groundwater; harms human health	Nitrates Directive monitoring surface waters that have high amounts of nitrates
Forests (during World War I)	deforestation	reforestation

Show What You Know

1. B
2. A
3. C
4. Clean Air Package
5. A, B, D
6. A, C
7. Answers may vary. Possible answers: After World War I, only around three percent of Britain's forests remained. To protect European forests, people passed laws to promote reforestation and made the cutting down of trees illegal in some areas.

Lesson Objectives

By the end of this lesson, your student will be able to:

• identify the physical processes that contribute to the availability and abundance of a natural resource

• compare and contrast the availability and distribution of natural resources in Europe across regions

Supporting Your Student

Read (Mining and Drilling)

As your student reads this section in the worktext, it may be helpful to retrieve a physical map of Europe by using an online search engine. For example, when your student learns about the European countries that are major producers of natural gas, such as Russia, Norway, the United Kingdom, and the Netherlands, have your student locate these countries on the map. Encourage your student to think about how physical processes, such as mining and drilling, affect the availability and abundance of natural resources, such as iron ore, across Europe.

Read (Aquaculture)

Help your student understand how fish are grown in aquaculture by using an online search engine to find video clips on how aquaculture works. Ask your student to identify unique features in aquaculture, such as the types of tanks that are used and the conditions that must be present in order for farmers to raise fish. As your student thinks through these questions, encourage them to dive deeper into the lesson and think about how the availability and distribution of natural resources like fish can impact Europe. For example, your student may identify that the Mediterranean Sea is rich in fish and allows for the distribution of fish to European countries. Your student may also suggest that the availability of natural resources may cause farmers to overfish and reduce the amount of fish in the sea, which is currently an issue in Europe.

Practice

Assist your student in filling in the bubble map by breaking up the task into smaller sections and focusing on the connections between the topics shown in the various bubbles. For example, first ask your student to identify the natural resources in Europe. Then ask your student to identify the physical objects that are used to retrieve natural resources. Finally, discuss the influence of availability and distribution of natural resources in Europe. For example, iron ore is abundant in Sweden, which produces 92 percent of Europe's supply. Due to the availability and abundance of iron ore in Sweden, it is frequently traded among European countries. However, the frequent mining of iron ore can release toxic substances in the environment, causing air and water pollution.

Learning Styles

Auditory learners may enjoy listening to a podcast on the types, availability, and distribution of natural resources in Europe.

Visual learners may enjoy watching a video clip on aquaculture and how it can influence the availability of fish in European seas.

Kinesthetic learners may enjoy drawing or creating models that represent the important natural resources in Europe, such as oil, natural gas, and fish.

Extension Activities

Visit a Local Farm

With your student, take a virtual or in-person trip to a local farm to learn more about aquaculture. Identify features of aquaculture, such as the types of fish, crustaceans, and aquatic plants that can be bred and raised. Encourage your student to examine the pros and cons of aquaculture and how it influences the availability, abundance, and distribution of natural resources in a region or around the world.

Create Your Own Jewelry

Have your student create jewelry pieces using beads, faux gems, or rhinestones to depict natural metals found in Europe (if items made of these elements are not available at home). For example, your student may be interested in creating a gold necklace. As your student designs the necklace, discuss the size, weight (in karats), and potential cost of the jewelry by investigating the recommended price per karat for gold. Encourage your student to also research how gold is mined by using an online search engine.

Answer Key

Write (How do mining and drilling influence the availability and abundance of natural resources in Europe?)

Answers will vary. Possible answers: Many natural resources, such as iron ore, are readily available in Europe. Sweden produces about 92 percent of Europe's iron ore, which is frequently traded among European countries and countries outside Europe, including China, the United States, and Turkey. Europe's supply of natural gas is primarily in Russia and is not always easy to access. To increase the availability of natural gas for distribution, Europe imports natural gas from regions in the Middle East.

Write (How does aquaculture influence the availability and distribution of fish in Europe?)

Answers will vary. Possible answers: The availability and frequent distribution of fish in European countries, such as Spain, Portugal, Sweden, and Norway, have caused farmers to overfish. It is estimated that bluefish tuna may become extinct in the Mediterranean by 2050.

Practice

Answers will vary. Possible answers:

1. Types of Natural Resources—gold, iron ore, oil, timber, natural gas
2. Types of Physical Processes—mining, drilling, aquaculture
3. Availability, Abundance, and Distribution—Iron ore in Sweden is available and abundant. It is frequently distributed among European countries to construct buildings and bridges.

Show What You Know

1. A
2. B, E
3. A, B, C
4. Answers will vary. Possible answers: Mining and drilling are processes that extract natural resources from the earth. Many natural resources, such as iron ore, are readily available in Europe. Sweden produces about 92 percent of Europe's iron ore, which is frequently traded among European countries and countries outside Europe, including China, the United States, and Turkey. Europe's supply of natural gas is primarily in Russia and is not always easy to access. To increase the availability of natural gas for distribution, Europe imports natural gas from regions in the Middle East.

Lesson Objectives

By the end of this lesson, your student will be able to:

- identify key natural resources found in Europe
- describe how the use, distribution, and importance of natural resources can affect different groups
- identify the impact of trade on the availability of natural resources

Supporting Your Student

Take a Closer Look

Your student may need to review terms such as *climate* and *temperate*. Discuss the reasons some types of fruits and vegetables might not grow in Europe. A temperate climate means Europe experiences warm summers and rainy winters with temperatures generally above freezing. The climate is also fairly arid, or dry. With fertile soil, many crops will grow in this type of environment, but tropical plants will not.

Explore

Draw your student's attention to the two pictures. Ask your student how these photos are similar and how they are different. These two pieces of technology (windmill and wind turbine) are very similar in form and purpose. Ask your student to look for and think about more examples of resources that Europeans have been using for long periods of time. How has the use or production of these resources changed over time?

Learning Styles

Auditory learners may enjoy listening to videos or podcasts on the importance of natural resources. Look for videos on the following topics:

- Agriculture in Europe
- Fishing in Europe
- Alternative energy in Europe
- Mining and drilling in Europe

Visual learners may enjoy drawing pictures of the key natural resources. Have the student fold a piece of paper into fourths and create an illustration of the four natural resources described. Your student can look up pictures of flags for the countries that a resource is abundant in and include the flags in the appropriate boxes.

Kinesthetic learners may enjoy finding objects around the home that can represent each key natural resource found in Europe. Ask the student why they choose a particular object to represent that key natural resource. Ask the student which country that key natural resource can be found in.

Extension Activities

Poster of a Country's Natural Resources

Have your student choose a country that has more than one key natural resource in Europe. Your student will create an art poster with a picture of the flag from that country and drawings of natural resources that are available in that chosen country. Label each natural resource drawn. Be sure to include the name of the country at the top of the page.

Europe's Natural Resources Mini Book

Have your student create a mini book. Your student can cut a sheet of paper into fourths and staple the pages together. Have them create a title page for the mini book, and then create a table of contents showing which natural resources are located on each page. On the content pages, have your student include the natural resource, a drawing of the natural resource printed from the computer or drawn, and countries where the natural resource is abundant.

Read *(Minerals and Energy)*

Utilizing a map for this section is recommended. As Russia's importance in providing fossil fuels to other European nations is discussed, point out that much of Russia is located on the continent of Asia. The Asian portion of Russia is sparsely populated. However, it is here that large deposits of fossil fuels have been found. Use the map to review the location of other countries that contain significant quantities of metals and fossil fuel.

Europe's Relationship with Natural Resources

Answer Key

Explore

Answers will vary. Possible answers: I think they will need to think creatively to come up with new ways to make energy and new ways to avoid using fossil fuels. Fossil fuels will not last forever. There is a limited amount of petroleum and natural gas, and they cause pollution.

Write *(How do migrant workers affect the natural resources in western Europe?)*

Answers will vary. Possible answer: Migrant workers help make agricultural resources available to European citizens. Without these migrant workers, countries such as France would have difficulty harvesting their crops.

Write *(What must many European countries rely on to ensure natural resources such as metal and fossil fuels are available?)*

Answers will vary. Possible answer: European countries must rely on trade with countries such as Russia for fossil fuels and Australia and South American countries for metals.

Practice

1. Natural gas, petroleum
2. Iron ore, natural gas
3. Wind energy, agricultural resources
4. Agricultural resources such as wheat, grapes, and cheese
5. Natural gas, wind energy, agricultural resources
6. Answers will vary. Possible answer: Countries in Europe trade their surplus resources for iron and fossil fuels. Without trade with countries such as Russia, Australia, and Brazil, Europe would not have the availability of resources it needs for the manufacture of automobiles.

Energy Debate *(Do you think countries should begin utilizing alternative forms of energy?)*

Answers will vary. Possible answer: I believe countries should begin utilizing alternative forms of energy because they would not need to import as many natural resources.

Show What You Know

1. Agricultural resources
2. Iron ore
3. C
4. A

In the Real World

Answers will vary. Possible answer: Fishing should be avoided in areas where bluefin tuna live to preserve the species. The fishing of species that are not in danger of extinction should be encouraged.

Lesson Objectives

By the end of this lesson, your student will be able to:

- explain how cultural attitudes, political unrest, economic downturns, and natural disasters influence the behavior of people in a region
- differentiate between voluntary and involuntary human migration
- identify the factors that led to the migration of people from one region in Europe to another
- describe the influences and contributions of the migrants to the new region

Supporting Your Student

Create
Ask your student if they hear different languages in their community. What languages do they hear? Help your student use these greetings. Challenge your student to use a new greeting each day. Ask your student how they would feel if they moved to a new country and did not speak the language. Do they think learning a new language would be difficult?

Explore
Talk to your student about the idea of cooperation. What does it mean to cooperate with other people? It means you need to work together, and you must agree on how to do something. Now imagine entire countries trying to cooperate with each other. They must agree on certain things to work together. The European Union has decided that democracy and a free-market economy are necessary if they are going to cooperate and make decisions together.

Read (Changes in Europe)
The idea of nationalism can be difficult to understand. Discuss the positive ways we can demonstrate loyalty to a country. Following laws and appreciating rights are wonderful ways to show you love your country. Singing a national anthem and flying your country's flag are other ways to show you love your country. Sometimes throughout history, countries have hurt other countries or communities to improve their own country or community's success. This is when the idea of nationalism can become a problem. Some of

Europe's countries decided it is better to cooperate and help each other, rather than just trying to help themselves.

Learning Styles

Auditory learners may enjoy listening to fairy tales or a short story from a culture other than their own. Ask your student what they really enjoyed about the story.

Visual learners may enjoy looking at art from a country other than their own. Consider taking a field trip to a local museum or do a virtual field trip to a museum. Talk about the different cultures that are depicted in the art.

Kinesthetic learners may enjoy learning a dance from a culture different from their own. Use a search engine to find different dances that your student could learn. Search "cultural dances."

Extension Activities

Migration Dilemma
Have your student select two European countries, one in the European Union (EU) and one not in the EU. To which country would they rather immigrate? Help your student create a Pros and Cons chart. On one side of the chart, list the pros, or reasons to move to a country in the European Union. On the other side, list cons, or reasons to move to a different country. Have your student write a complete sentence explaining their final decision.

Create a Brochure
Have your student create a brochure that encourages immigrants to move to their neighborhood. Ask your student leading questions: "What attractive things do you have in your neighborhood that you would like to advertise? How would you make newcomers feel welcome? What can you teach them about your neighborhood or city?"

Answer Key

Explore
Answers will vary. Possible answers: Some countries may not want to follow the same rules other nations do. They may not want to trade freely or allow migration. They may want to use their own currency. Countries might feel they can be more successful on their own. Some countries might not be allowed to join the union because their governments are difficult to work and compromise with.

Write *(How has Europe changed since the formation of the European Union?)*
Answers will vary. Possible answer: Members of the European Union cooperate and strive to avoid conflicts with each other.

Write *(What are some causes of involuntary migration?)*
Answers will vary. Possible answers: jobs, political unrest, natural disasters

Practice *(Why do populations migrate during periods of recession?)*
Answers will vary. Possible answer: Populations need economic opportunities to pay for the resources they need.

Show What You Know
1. False
2. True
3. False
4. Answers will vary. Possible answer: They provide labor, innovations, and culture.

Online Connection
Answers will vary. Possible answer: I think the stars represent the countries in the European Union. I was wrong! The flag represents Europe as a whole.

Lesson Objectives

By the end of this lesson, your student will be able to:

- identify the location of key cultural features and relate their significance
- relate how cultural features in a region influence population, the economy, government, and transportation

Supporting Your Student

Create

Use this opportunity to help your student build an understanding of culture and the different aspects of culture. Prompt your student to identify different aspects of their culture, such as language, religion, traditions, holidays, and foods. Give your student options for creating exhibits for their museum. They can use photographs, illustrations, or artifacts (items they find at home).

Explore

Ask your student if they have ever traveled as a tourist. What did they do while they were on vacation? Did they spend money where they visited? Tell your student that if a region is popular with tourists, it receives money from these visitors. This strengthens the economy. Review the word *economy* with your student. A region's economy is their wealth or ability to buy, use, and sell resources.

Read (Changing Cultural Features)

Help your student understand the ideas in this section by pointing out that ideas change over time. For example, in the past, women were not allowed to vote in many countries, but today women hold the same rights as men in many countries. As public opinions change, the culture changes too.

Learning Styles

Auditory learners may enjoy listening to music from different cultures throughout Europe. Your student may enjoy listening to various languages throughout Europe.

Visual learners may enjoy drawing a picture of a famous piece of art from Europe. Use a search engine to look up famous pieces of art from different countries in Europe. Encourage your student to look for pictures from the country they are studying. Have them draw, paint, and/or color the same picture. Be sure to include the artist's name on the piece of work.

Kinesthetic learners may enjoy dressing up as a person from a different European country. Use a search engine to look up ways different cultures dress in different countries in Europe. Encourage your student to be creative using their own clothing to mirror how the chosen culture dresses. Kinesthetic learners may enjoy acting out different etiquette practices from European culture.

Extension Activities

Landmark Research

Tell your student that landmarks are important places or monuments that are culturally significant. The Eiffel Tower, Pompeii, the Leaning Tower of Pisa, the Colosseum, Big Ben, Stonehenge, and the Arc de Triomphe are all examples of famous landmarks. Have your student select one of Europe's famous landmarks and research why it is important or significant to its country's culture.

Take a Field Trip

Take a field trip to a local museum so your student can experience local art. Consider taking a virtual field trip through one of the country's important buildings, such as the White House or the Capitol Building.

Answer Key

Explore

Answers will vary. Possible answer: Tourists spend money in the countries they visit. This brings money to different economies.

Write (How has religion influenced life in Europe?)

Answers will vary. Possible answer: Christian traditions throughout Europe have influenced architecture. Many churches throughout Europe are maintained and restored even though it is very expensive to do so. Populations attend church regularly, and tourists visit churches.

Write (How are some cultural features changing in Europe?)

Answers will vary. Possible answers: Some cities with cobblestone streets are removing the cobblestones to pave the streets in asphalt and cement. Some museums are considering returning art from countries that were colonized long ago.

Practice

Answers will vary. Possible answers:

Cultural Feature	Description and Influence in Europe
Christianity	The most popular religion in Europe is Christianity. Churches throughout Europe are visited regularly. Vatican City, the center of Catholicism, is located in Italy.
Democracy	Democracy, or a government that allows the people to vote, is the dominant form of government throughout Europe.
Art	Many art museums have been built throughout Europe. They show that Europe values art and artists.
Architecture	Old buildings and structures can be seen throughout Europe. Governments and communities spend time and money on preserving historical buildings.
Channel Tunnel	In Europe, citizens enjoy visiting other countries. The tunnel that connects England and France allows migrants and tourists easy passage between these two countries.
Cobblestone Roads	Cobblestone roads in Europe are extremely old. Many people enjoy experiencing history every time they walk down the street. Some of these roads are being replaced.

Show What You Know

1. B
2. A
3. C
4. Answers will vary. Possible answer: There are many museums throughout Europe. People travel throughout Europe to visit these museums and celebrate famous artists.

Create (What food is part of your culture?)

Answers will vary. Possible answer: My family makes pasta. This tradition has been passed down through the generations. My grandmother is Italian and learned how to make pasta from her mother.

Lesson Objectives

By the end of this lesson, your student will be able to:

- investigate the cultural geography of Europe
- explore broader influences of European culture on individuals and civilizations around the world
- discover the lasting impact of European culture on everyday aspects of life

Supporting Your Student

Practice

After your student completes the chart, have them highlight aspects that they think have changed the world in the Europe's Influence column. The cultural influence that has the most descriptions highlighted could be the influence that the student chooses to write about in the Write section. They can use the items they highlighted as evidence to support their claim.

Learning Styles

Auditory learners may enjoy listening to different styles of music from various cultures or countries in Europe. Your student can use a search engine to look up music from France, Belgium, Italy, and so forth. Ask your student if they recognize any of these styles of music from their own country.

Visual learners may also enjoy looking at different works of art from countries in Europe. Take a virtual tour through famous museums online, such as the Louvre in Paris, France.

Kinesthetic learners may enjoy acting out a game of charades for the various cultural influences. Take turns acting out a cultural influence. Determine what the cultural influence is, or if you act out a specific contribution, which cultural influence would it be categorized as. Make sure to ask how the behavior relates to the cultural geography of Europe and the influence it has around the world. For example, your student may act out putting on eyeglasses to read.

Extension Activities

Make a Multimedia Presentation

Direct your student to choose four or five of their favorite inventions. Tell your student to create a multimedia presentation. Your student should provide information on each of the chosen inventions. They should provide a picture for each invention. Tell your student to answer the following questions for each chosen invention:

1. What country was this invention created in?
2. Who was responsible for creating this invention?
3. When was this invention created?

Greek Alphabet Flip Book

Your student can create a flip book of the Greek alphabet. There should be one page for each letter in the Greek alphabet. Tell your student to be sure that the symbol for the letter and the letter are included on the page.

Greek Alphabet Flash Cards

Your student can create flash cards to practice and learn the Greek alphabet. Your student should be sure that the symbol for the letter is on one side of the card. The other side of the card should have the letter that the symbol stands for. They can then practice learning each symbol and letter.

Answer Key

Write (What is one specific way that the world has benefited from the cultural geography of Europe?)

Answers will vary. Possible answers: The world has benefited from the cultural geography of Europe through advancements in technology, such as eyeglasses that help people see and read and gunpowder that helps military missions. Another way the world has benefited from Europe's cultural geography is the development of the scientific process in science.

Practice

Answers will vary. Possible answers:

Category	Europe's Influence
Architecture	Cathedrals would not be as artistic and dramatic as they are.
	There would not be a Gothic style of architecture.
	Medieval castles would not exist, which could change how certain battles were won in history.
Arts	Paintings would not emphasize emotion.
	Parts of history may not be preserved as they are in art.
	People would not understand each other's cultures as well because of art.
Communication	We would not read or write from left to right.
Culinary	We would not have dry pasta.
Science	We would not have the scientific process.
Technology	People would not have eyeglasses.
	Military would not have gunpowder.

Show What You Know

1. B, D
2. A, B, C, D, E, F, G
3. True
4. F
5. A
6. H
7. G
8. B
9. I
10. J
11. E
12. C
13. D
14. Answers will vary. Possible answer: Cultural geography is the study of human connection to natural resources, the economy, religion, government, and many other ways that humans interact with their world.

Lesson Objectives

By the end of this lesson, your student will review the following big ideas from Chapter 4.

- Different maps of Europe can tell us different stories about the continent. (Lesson 33)
- Europe has many geographic features throughout. (Lesson 34)
- Human settlement had patterns in Europe. (Lesson 35)
- There are different physical geography and natural resources throughout Europe. (Lesson 36)
- Humans have had an impact on the environment in Europe. (Lesson 37)
- There are different physical processes in Europe, and they impact the natural resources. (Lesson 38)
- Europe has a relationship with the natural resources on the continent. (Lesson 39)
- There were different migration patterns caused by different factors in Europe. (Lesson 40)
- There are many cultural features of Europe. (Lesson 41)
- Cultural geography in Europe has influenced the rest of the world in many ways. (Lesson 42)

Supporting Your Student

Practice *(Four's a Crowd)*
For assistance with this activity, allow your student to refer back to the lessons to find answers and relationships among words. Have your student use a process of elimination. To do this, your student will mark out words that they know are similar or associated with the other words. They will most likely understand two words that relate easily without having to dig deeper. Have them cross those two words off first, and then research within the chapter to find the remaining two words and the relationship to the others.

Practice *(Cause and Effect)*
For assistance with this activity, allow your student to refer back to the lessons to find answers. This activity could push your student a little more. Remind your student that there is not only one cause to each effect. Likewise, there is also not only one effect to each cause. Therefore, multiple answers that your student comes up with could be considered correct. Allow your student to skip around and answer some of the easier cause and effect questions. Once they get the gist, they should feel more comfortable attacking some of the harder cause and effect questions.

Practice *(Positives and Negatives)*
For assistance with this activity, allow your student to refer back to the lessons to find answers. Allow your student to read each topic. It is likely that they will have some ideas about various positives and negatives for different topics before referring back to the lesson content. Allow students to fill in what they know first. Then, with whatever is left, remind your student to read headings in the lessons to help them find more positives and negatives.

Learning Styles

Auditory learners may enjoy listening to a podcast on interesting facts about Europe. This will allow your student to understand Europe more effectively. Use a search engine to search "*Podcasts on facts about Europe for kids.*"

Visual learners may enjoy watching a video on facts about Europe. Use a search engine to look up a video. Search "*Video on Europe for kids*" on a video streaming service online. Ask your student for three things that stood out to them during this video.

Kinesthetic learners may enjoy gathering objects around the home that relate to the story of Europe. Have your student search for at least five objects that somehow relate to the story of Europe and facts they have learned throughout this unit of study. When they return with the objects, have them hold the object and ask them how it relates to what they learned.

Extension Activities

Create a Collage

Your student can use a multimedia presentation tool to create a collage of aspects about Europe that they learned about. Your student should write a caption for each picture. They should include a minimum of 10 pictures in the collage.

Summary Chapter Book

Your student can make a book that provides key bullet points for each chapter. Each page of the book should include a page for each lesson in the unit. On each page, your student should include a title, at least one picture, and at least four bulleted points that stood out to them in the lesson. Your student can create a table of contents too. This could be handwritten, or it could be created using a word processing tool on the computer.

Answer Key

Write (Explain when you would use a geopolitical map, a topographic map, and a tourist map.)

Answers will vary. Possible answers: Geopolitical—If you want to know where the boundary of a new country is, you would use a geopolitical map. Topographic—If you are hiking and want to go to the highest peak in a country, you would want a topographic map. Tourist—When you are traveling to a new country and want to know what you should see, you would want a tourist map.

Write (Describe at least two ways the geography of Europe benefits the European people.)

Answers will vary. Possible answer: The mountains benefit Europeans because they provide protection from invaders. Glaciers benefit Europeans because they provide clean water and assist with hydropower.

Practice (Four's a Crowd)

Answers will vary. Possible answers:

Circle the word that does not belong.	Explain why that word does not belong.
Mexico City	All the other words are major cities in Europe.
plains	All the other geographic features involve water.
vast deserts	All the other geographic features are found throughout Europe.
fish	All the other natural resources require mining.
volcanoes	The others are innovative ways to access energy without harming the environment.
landscape	All the other words are ways that migrants influenced Europe.
tourists	Migration can be voluntary or involuntary.
natural disasters	All words are causes of migration, but natural disasters are not caused by humans.

Practice *(Cause and Effect)*
Answers will vary. Possible answer:

Cause	Effect
Wars occur, reformations occur, and empires change power.	Boundaries to countries on a map change.
Timber, an important natural resource in Europe, was used for WWI in the United Kingdom.	Timber is a natural resource that was overused and is now in need in the United Kingdom.

Cause	Effect
The physical process of erosion occurs often in Europe.	Soil can become more fertile, but water can become more contaminated.
One human settlement pattern in Europe was to settle near mountains.	By people settling near this geographic feature, they were offered protection from invaders and rich, fertile soil for growing food.

Cause	Effect
Some Europeans refused to convert to Catholicism.	They would be forced to migrate to other parts of Europe, or they would be killed.
Humans migrated to different countries throughout Europe.	Art, communications, architecture, and transportation improved in Europe.

Practice *(Positives and Negatives)*
Answers will vary. Possible answers:

Topic: There are many different geographic features in Europe.	
Positives	**Negatives**
Different geographic features helped humans with settlement, such as lakes or rivers. The geographic feature of mountains protected humans from invaders.	Some geographic features, such as mountains, can make trading difficult. Some geographic features, such as deserts, are difficult areas for humans to settle.

Topic: Natural resources are being used often by Europeans.	
Positives	**Negatives**
People are coming up with innovative ways to save our natural resources. Natural resources were used to trade with other countries and often benefited the country that had the natural resource in abundance.	Some natural resources began to run out. Getting to natural resources sometimes causes damage to the environment, such as during the process of mining.

Topic: Migration occurred throughout Europe.	
Positives	**Negatives**
Migrants made positive changes to the cultural geography of places they moved to. Migration made people safer in some instances, or it gave them a better job and financial situation.	People were sometimes forced to migrate involuntarily. Some empires, like the Roman Empire, forced people to migrate if they didn't convert to a certain religion.

Quick Review

Refer to the statement your student circled in the Show What You Know section to self-assess their knowledge of the chapter concepts. Then to assist in determining if your student is ready to take the assessment, consider:

- Having your student point to maps that are topographic, tourist, and geopolitical and explain the differences between them.
- Having your student explain what the geographic features of Europe and use a map to identify and explain characteristics of each geographic feature.
- Having your student describe the main physical geography on the continent of Europe and explain how these features impacted human settlement.
- Having your student describe what natural resources are found on the continent of Europe.
- Having your student explain the main cultural features found on the continent of Europe.

Discover! SOCIAL STUDIES • GRADE 5 • CHAPTER 4 ASSESSMENT

113

Chapter Assessment

Label each map of Europe with what kind of map it is.

1. _____

2. _____

3. _____

4. Which of these geographic features are in Europe? Circle all that apply.

A. glaciers

B. mountains

C. roads

D. oceans

5. Explain two different patterns of human settlement in Europe.

....

....

6. List four geographic features found in Europe.

....

....

....

....

7. List five different natural resources found throughout Europe.

....

....

....

....

....

8. In what ways do humans have an impact on the environment in Europe? Circle all that apply.

A. overusing natural resources

B. underusing natural resources

C. innovative ways to help replenish natural resources

D. ignoring their negative impacts on natural resources

9. Below each physical process in Europe, describe one impact it has on natural resources.

A. Volcano

....

....

B. Glacier

....

....

10. Explain two ways that Europe has a relationship with natural resources.

....

....

11. Which statement describes the different migration patterns in Europe?

   A. Migration in Europe was always voluntary.

   B. Migration in Europe was always involuntary.

   C. Migration in Europe was involuntary and voluntary.

   D. Migration in Europe did not occur.

12. True or False   There are not many cultural features in Europe.

13. In what way has cultural geography in Europe influenced the rest of the world?

   A. Cultural geography in Europe has not influenced the rest of the world.

   B. Cultural geography in Europe has influenced a small part of the world.

   C. Cultural geography in Europe has had a significant influence on the rest of the world.

   D. Cultural geography in Europe has influenced about half the world.

Chapter Assessment Answer Key

1. tourist

2. geopolitical

3. topographic

4. A, B, D

5. Answers will vary. Possible answer: Human settlement began in Europe thousands of years ago. Humans began migrating to Europe from Africa and the Middle East. Cold environments in Europe motivated humans to continue migrating to warmer climates in eastern Europe, where they could practice agriculture and raise livestock. Humans left Africa to escape the drying climate. Mountain ranges offered protection from invaders and had rich soil for growing crops. Scandinavia, a region in northern Europe, was settled by the Sami culture, due to the presence of reindeer herds.

6. Answers will vary. Possible answers: mountains, ocean, desert, lakes, channels, canals, glaciers, foothills, plateaus

7. Answers will vary. Possible answers: fish, water, silver, walrus ivory, coal, petroleum, horses, timber, agriculture, gold, silver, grapes, marble, clay, ore

8. A, C

9. A. creates fertile soil

B. creates water source, can produce hydropower

10. Answers will vary. Possible answers: Resources such as timber have been overused. Europeans are working to reverse damage to natural resources by coming up with innovative ways to help, like hydropower.

11. C

12. False

13. C

Alternative Assessment

Project: For this project, you will create a poster with four maps of Europe that each tell a different story about the continent.

Project Requirements or Steps:

1. Divide a poster board into four sections.

2. Print or sketch four different maps of Europe for each section.

3. Label each section: Early Settlement, Natural Resources, Geographic Features, Cultural Features

4. Include the following on each map:

- Early Settlement
    - Label where three different groups settled
    - Label the four regions of Europe
    - Label at least three major cities in Europe
    - Create a key with labels
- Natural Resources
    - Label five different natural resources and the country they are found in
    - Create a key with labels
- Geographic Features
    - Label at least four different geographic features
    - Create a key with labels
- Cultural Features
    - Label at least four different cultural features found throughout Europe
    - Include the name of the cultural feature, the city, and the country
    - Create a key with labels

5. Share your poster with friends and family.

Alternative Assessment Rubric

Use the following rubric to grade your student's assessment.

	4	3	2	1	Points
Connection to the Chapter	The project is clearly connected to the chapter.	The project is connected to the chapter.	The project is somewhat connected to the chapter.	The project is not connected to the chapter.	
Creativity	The project is very creative and aesthetically appealing.	The project is creative and aesthetically appealing.	The project is somewhat creative and aesthetically appealing.	The project is not creative or aesthetically appealing.	
Information	The information or data is very accurate and easy to follow.	The information or data is accurate.	The information or data is somewhat accurate.	The information or data is not accurate.	
Grammar and Mechanics	There are no grammar and punctuation mistakes.	There are one or two grammar and punctuation mistakes.	There are several grammar and punctuation mistakes.	There are a distracting number of grammar and punctuation mistakes.	

Total Points _____/16

Average _____

Lesson Objectives

By the end of this lesson, your student will be able to:

• identify different types of maps of North America
• determine a story each map tells
• compare and contrast the major cities in North America and the cities in your state or country

Supporting Your Student

Read *(Topography in North America)*

Your student will be exploring a topographical map in this section. They might have difficulty with seeing a topographical map in a photo form. Describe how different parts of the map may feel with respect to depth and height if you were able to feel the texture shown by the colors and shading. For example, the brown areas would feel bumpy and higher because of the mountains. The green areas would feel smooth and low because of the plains.

Write *(Compare your hometown to one of the cities on this page. Write one way they are alike and one way they are different.)*

Your student may have difficulty finding comparisons to the cities discussed in the text if you do not live in a big city. Consider going online or looking in a print atlas to find other cities or towns that are more similar to where you live. Alternatively, you could encourage your student to think about things that most cities have in common, like city parks, libraries, grocery stores, and a post office.

Write *(What story can you tell about North America from looking at the geopolitical map?)*

Help your student determine a story for the map by having them point to the different countries and name them. Then, ask your student to look at the area of each country. Which is biggest? Which is smallest? Ask your student to think about why Alaska, which is part of the United States, is located so far from the rest of the country. This is a perfect opportunity to talk about how countries might create agreements selling or giving land to one another, just as Alaska was purchased from Russia.

Learning Styles

Auditory learners may enjoy writing a song to tell a story about a map or about their hometown.

Visual learners may enjoy researching additional types of maps to gain more perspective on the view of North America. They could look up tourist maps, city maps, or road maps.

Kinesthetic learners may enjoy creating their own topographical map of their area of the world or of North America by using clay or other textured materials.

Extension Activities

Another Kind of Map

Introduce a population density map. A population density map is a map of the number of people for a given area. Have your student explore where they notice the most people live. Engage in a discussion about how the impact of population affects the environment. Discuss the reasons people might have for choosing where to live. Discuss why your family chooses to live where they live.

Create a Continent

Have your student create their own continent. Tell your student their work is to think about the geographical landscape of their continent. What types of landforms will it have? Then, have your student create a topographical map of the continent. They could use color and shading to show the topography or they could use clay or other textured materials. Are the landforms tourist attractions? If so, they could also create a tourist map.

Answer Key

Explore

Answers will vary. Possible answers: I notice mountains and rivers. I wonder what types of water are found in my city (or country).

Write *(What story does this map tell about the United States?)*

Answers will vary. Possible answer: The map tells the story of a country with different types of land and water. The western part has a lot of mountains, which might be difficult to travel through. The eastern part has a lot of plains, which might be easier to travel through.

Write *(Compare your hometown to one of the cities on this page. Write one way they are alike and one way they are different.)*

Answers will vary greatly depending on your student's hometown.

Write *(What story can you tell about North America from looking at the geopolitical map?)*

Answers will vary. Possible answer: I can tell that North America seems to have three main areas: Canada, United States, and an area shown in blue that has Mexico and other countries. It seems that the United States is divided into a lot more states than Canada. Also, it appears that the United States has states that are not connected to the rest of the states and one of them looks like an island.

Show What You Know

1. B
2. A
3. Answers will vary. Possible answer: The landform is mountain ranges. It might tell you that the west is a rugged place and that it is a difficult place to live, or it might tell you that the west is a fun place because the mountains provide a lot of entertainment.
4. B
5. Answers will vary depending on where your student lives.

Lesson Objectives

By the end of this lesson, your student will be able to:

- analyze geographic factors that influence where people live and how people came to settle North America
- develop spatial understanding of the location of geographic features in North America to those studied in previous chapters
- identify geographic connections between the continents

Supporting Your Student

Explore

In this lesson, your student is being prepared to understand how the geographic features of the land impacted the settlers that arrived in North America. People were promised a wonderful land, but were quite shocked when they arrived in North America. In this section, you can help your student by explaining to them how arriving in America wasn't as the settlers expected it to be. You can ask them to think about a time when something didn't go as they expected it to. What did they do? How did they handle the situation?

Write *(What problems and benefits would there be for Alaska and Russia to be so close at the Bering Strait?)*

Your student will need to think about the problems that could result when two countries that do not always get along are close to each other. Also, they might think about how countries being so close together could help each other. Ask your student, "How might countries not get along if they are close together?" and "How might two countries help each other since they are located so close together?"

Practice

In this activity, your student is comparing and contrasting. This is a skill of identifying similarities and differences. To guide your student through this comparison, have them think beyond the fact that the two straits are on separate continents. They should think about how the straits are used, the land masses in between the two, the safety of the waters there, the depth of the water, and other features of the straits.

Learning Styles

Auditory learners may enjoy listening to stories of people traveling to North America on ships. Your student may enjoy hearing about what their conditions were like on the way to North America and what they saw when they arrived there. You can find examples of this online.

Visual learners may enjoy viewing charts and maps comparing North America to other continents. Some types they could look at are population and economic maps.

Kinesthetic learners may enjoy creating a scene of what a settlement looked like when people arrived in North America by acting it out.

Extension Activities

Compare It

In this activity, your student will pick a specific continent with which to compare North America. They should research the population, size of the continent, famous landmarks, number of countries within the continent, and number of languages spoken in the continent. They may include other facts that they find interesting. Your student can display their comparison in the way that works best for their learning style. Options for display can include charts, Venn diagrams, or essays.

Traveling to America

In this activity, your student will select one family (or they may create their own) that traveled from another continent to America. They will research how the family traveled to America, what hardships they faced when they arrived, where they chose to settle and how they got along while learning to live and survive in a new area. If your student chooses to create their own fictional family, they should be sure to include the number of people in the family, what belongings they have, and how they got along while learning to live and survive in the new area. Your student can display this work in a variety of formats. Options for display can include a storybook, essay, or artwork.

Answer Key

In the Real World

Answers will vary. Possible answer: This is where our extended family members live. One (or both) of my parents found a better job here. There are more opportunities here for work, better education, etc.

Explore

Answers will vary. Possible answer: I will need to find someplace to live and a job. I will need shelter, food, and a job.

Write (What problems and benefits would there be for Alaska and Russia to be so close at the Bering Strait?)

Answers will vary. Possible answer: They could help each other by trading. A problem could be that both sides want to fish in the same area and they must share it.

Practice

Answers will vary. Possible answer:

Bering Strait
Formed by glaciers
Very cold
Very shallow

Both
Narrow straits that form into smaller seas
Strong currents

Strait of Gibraltar
Formed by tectonic plate movement
Very deep
Very warm

Show What You Know

1. C
2. C
3. B
4. B
5. B
6. D
7. C

Lesson Objectives

By the end of this lesson, your student will be able to:

- examine evidence of common patterns and features of human settlements
- compare and contrast human settlements of different regions in North America
- analyze how the environment influenced human settlements

Supporting Your Student

Explore

Your student will explore different types of settlements. As they engage with the lesson, your student should recognize that settlements come in all different shapes and sizes. In this activity, your student is entertaining the idea that they could build a house out of anything! Show them examples of homes people built out of school buses, airplanes, and more. Help your student imagine these homes by showing them pictures of homes people have built out of unique materials. Ask them to think about any object they might want to build a house out of. If they prefer a traditional home, then vary the location of where the home might be built. Would they consider it on the water? High up on a mountaintop?

Read *(Common Patterns in Human Settlements)*

Your student is gathering a lot of information about the types of settlements. They would benefit from keeping track of the definitions of the different types of settlements (village/hamlet, town, suburb, city, metropolis). Have them think about the area where they live and describe it by size. Have them record their response so they can create a personal frame of reference.

Learning Styles

Auditory learners may enjoy listening to stories of farmers or city workers discussing the importance of their roles in their respective areas.

Visual learners may enjoy researching additional images of the types of settlements.

Kinesthetic learners may enjoy creating a three-dimensional structure of their region or hometown showing the settlement of the area.

Extension Activities

Model Home

Your student was asked to write about a home they would build if they could use any material they wished. Provide your student with the opportunity to draw or build a model of that home. They could use materials like clay or popsicle sticks to build models of their home designs. Encourage your student to describe their homes and even label major components of it.

Create a Regions of North America Map

Use a search engine to find maps of the eight regions of North America by searching "Eight Regions of North America Map." If possible, print the map and color it. If you cannot print the map, have your student draw a map of North America and sketch out where each region would be located according to the descriptions provided.

Answer Key

Explore *(Imagine you were told you could build any kind of house you wanted. What would you build? Where would you build it? Why do you think people choose to live in different types of homes and in different places?)*

Answers will vary. Your student's answer should creatively consider different materials to use to build a house that reflect available resources in an area.

Write *(How do you think your area was settled? What features in your area make you think this?)*

Answers will vary based on the region your student lives in. Your student's answer should reflect an understanding of the lesson. Possible answer: I think my area was settled because of how close it is to a river. While I do not live very close to a river, there is a major river that is less than an hour's drive from my house.

Write *(What environmental factors influence where people settle in North America?)*

Answers will vary. Possible answers: climate, access to water, ability to raise livestock or grow crops

Practice *(Regional Settlements)*

Region	Do many people live in this region? What is the main reason?
1. Coastal Range	Yes. Answers will vary, but climate and trade are strong answers.
2. Basin and Range	No. Answers will vary, but few resources is a strong answer.
3. Rocky Mountains	No. Answers will vary, but difficult terrain is a strong answer.
4. Great Plains	No or Some. Answers will vary, but weather is a strong answer.
5. Interior Lowlands	Yes. Answers will vary, but resources and agriculture are strong answers.
6. Canadian Shield	No. Answers will vary, but climate or poor agriculture are strong answers.
7. Appalachian Mountains	No or Some. Answers will vary, but difficult terrain is a strong answer.
8. Coastal Plain	Yes. Answers will vary. Almost any answer will have merit.

Show What You Know

1. B
2. Answers will vary. Possible answers: Rivers are a source of transportation and food. Students may remember that annual flooding renews the soil, which is why civilization began in river valleys (Nile, Mesopotamia, Indus, Yangtze, etc.).
3. Answers will vary. Possible answers: Harsh winters make it hard to grow crops. Lots of water makes it easier to grow crops and raise livestock. Water also makes it easy for trade. Dry areas lack water, which would make it hard to grow crops or raise livestock.

Lesson Objectives

By the end of this lesson, your student will be able to:

- describe the physical geography of North America
- analyze the effects of other people's use of natural resources on the development of various Indigenous North American civilizations

Supporting Your Student

Explore

As your student enters this lesson, they have learned that water serves an important purpose in geography. They have learned that water is used as a source for transportation and trading. Your student is being asked to think about the impact of water differently. Help your student understand that creating your own reservoirs, or holding tanks of water, means that people would be able to have access to water in any place they wanted.

Read

Your student is gaining a lot of knowledge as they read through this lesson. Support your student by encouraging good note-taking strategies like highlighting, keeping a vocabulary journal, and writing summaries of key information. You might also share the brain dump and mind-mapping strategies with your student. Mind maps are freeform visual representations of information. Your student can be as creative as the like in creating this type of graphic organizer. A brain dump is when you immediately record everything you can remember when you're done reading or studying something. Combining these two strategies following information-dense reading increases retention exponentially.

Your student might need support fully connecting to the ways European settlement had an impact on Indigenous tribal nations' ways of life. You can ask guiding questions like, "How did tribal nations hunt before settlers came in?" "How would the presence of European settlers change the way they hunted?" "Some tribal nations were semi-nomadic or entirely nomadic, moving with the seasons to access resources. How would settlers claiming lands for themselves change that?"

Learning Styles

Auditory learners may enjoy listening to selections from the audiobook of *Life on the Mississippi*.

Visual learners may enjoy exploring maps of Indigenous tribal nations to see what regions of North America they inhabited.

Kinesthetic learners may enjoy creating models of the Native American homes or one of the Mayan Temples.

Extension Activities

Steamboats

The Mississippi River is famous for its steamboats. The steamboats were important during the nineteenth century as they allowed for large scale transport of goods and people. Have your student research the Mississippi River steamboats and the impact they had (and still have) on the Mississippi River area.

Native American Tribal Nations

As your student learned, there are hundreds of Native American tribes. Have your student research the tribal nations that inhabited the lands closest to their home. Ask them to learn about where the tribe was located, what they ate and how they used the land to help themselves. Your student can present this work in a written or oral report using photographs to show the information they learned.

Answer Key

Explore

Answers will vary. Possible answer: If I were very thirsty, getting water would be exciting. A well would mean water would be easier to get from then on. Water is important because it is necessary for survival. Indoor plumbing is common, I get water from a sink, and I can get bottled water at a store.

Show What You Know

1. False
2. False
3. True
4. reservoirs
5. Answers will vary. Possible answers: weaving baskets from grass, making baskets from birchbark, making canoes from birchbark, weaving beds from grass, making pottery from mud, making cooking pots from mud, making shelter out of available materials, sourcing food from the land or ocean, using the mountains for protection, constructing roads

Lesson Objectives

By the end of this lesson, your student will be able to:

- identify ways people make changes and respond to changes to their environment
- analyze the reasons for the establishment of the Mississippi River and Tributaries Project and describe the Army Corps of Engineers' role in controlling Mississippi River flooding
- identify other ways that people in North America made changes to their environment
- illustrate examples of how they responded to changes in the environment

Supporting Your Student

Explore

Your student is being given an aerial perspective of the land, recognizing that a bird coasting on water would not run into a tree and certainly not a vehicle. If your student needs support, point them in the direction of the photo. Ask them if they would typically see water on a city street like in the photo. Guide them in a discussion of what could cause water to become on city streets.

Practice

Your student has gained a lot of information about the Great Flood of 1927. In the reading section, they learned about the events that led up to the flood and how it was hoped that the levees and floodways would repair it. If your student finds it difficult to put the events in order, guide them back to the reading and have them highlight or underline the important events. Ask them then to recite the events back to you in order. Then, go back to the practice section and have them complete the sequencing activity.

Write *(Deforestation changes the environment. What are the major impacts of deforestation?)*

As your student explores how physical environmental changes can negatively impact the environment, see if you can refer to any physical environmental changes that you noticed within your own community, like land being cleared to make space for new buildings. When your student has the opportunity to make the connection to their own hometown or region, they will be able to connect with the negative impacts more readily.

Learning Styles

Auditory learners may enjoy listening to historical accounts of people who experienced the Great Flood of 1927.

Visual learners may enjoy additional photographs depicting the Great Flood of 1927 or watching videos to see the historical effects on the land. Visual learners may also enjoy drawing before and after pictures of a physical change in their own hometown or area, like the construction of new shopping malls or restaurants.

Kinesthetic learners may enjoy planting a new tree, bush, or their favorite flowers near their home.

Extension Activities

Effect of Great Flood of 1927 on Music

As your student learned, the Great Flood of 1927 was a landmark event in American history. The flooding left damage to more than ten states and to hundreds of thousands of people. Even when the water receded, the effect on the people remained. During this time, people turned to writing music and singing songs about the events that occurred. Have your student research and listen to the songs of the time. Ask them to select one that they find the most inspirational and then have them write about the meaning of the song.

Build a Floodway

As your student learned, building levees and floodways were crucial to controlling the flooding of the Mississippi River. Ask your student to create their own river, either through use of real materials and water, or by drawing. Ask them to show how they would control the flooding of their created river.

Answer Key

Practice
2, 5, 1, 3, 4

Write *(Deforestation changes the environment. What are the major impacts of deforestation?)*
Answers will vary. Possible answers: Animals might leave an area because their homes no longer exist. Rodents could move into human populated areas and cause disease. The ecosystem can become destabilized. Caribou have lost part of their habitat. There is increased air pollution and increased flooding.

Show What You Know
1. True
2. C
3. A, B, D
4. C
5. Answers will vary. Possible answers: oil and resource mining, road building, transportation or recreation
6. Answers will vary. Possible answer: It gave power to the Army Corps of Engineers to control the flooding of the Mississippi River.

Lesson Objectives

By the end of this lesson, your student will be able to:

- identify examples of physical processes that contribute to the availability and abundance of a natural resource
- compare and contrast the availability and distribution of natural resources in North America across regions

Supporting Your Student

Read (Appalachian Mountains)

As your student is reading about the natural resources found in the environment, they might find confusion with the subject of mining. If mining is a topic your student is unfamiliar with, take a moment to research and explore the process of mining from text resources or online. Engage your student in a discussion of how the process of mining is difficult, the equipment is costly, and that mining can sometimes be dangerous. As they explore the concept of mining, engage them in a discussion of why certain regions of North America would be better suited for mining than others.

Practice

As your student explores the similarities and differences between plate tectonics and plate collisions, it would be helpful to search online for a video showing how each of those formations is different. Your student may also enjoy using pieces of paper to then demonstrate for you the difference between plate tectonics and plate collision.

Read (Regions in North America)

As your student explores the different regions of North America, it would be helpful if you used an online search engine to search for a map of "the eight regions of North America." As your student is reading the text, stop them after each region to point out where in North America each of these regions are.

Learning Styles

Auditory learners may enjoy listening to stories of coal miners and how they do their work.

Visual learners may enjoy watching videos of volcanic eruptions or underground coal mining.

Kinesthetic learners may enjoy creating an underwater volcano and forcing it up to the water surface to build an island.

Extension Activities

Create a Brochure

It isn't just Hawaii that was formed by volcanic activity. In fact, Yellowstone is another popular area that was formed by volcanic activity. Have your student research how Yellowstone was formed and create a travel brochure to invite tourists to come and learn the history. The brochure should include how Yellowstone was formed, what its activity level is today and how it compares to the past, and its popularity as a tourist location.

Write a Speech

Your student has learned about erosion in previous lessons. The Grand Canyon was formed by the Colorado River. It attests to the strength of the Colorado River. Have your student research more about how the Grand Canyon was formed and how erosion contributed to its formation. Have your student prepare a speech that details the formation of the Grand Canyon.

Answer Key

Practice

Answers will vary. Possible answers:

	Similarities	Differences
Hawaii	formed by the movement of Earth	volcanic activity shifted the plates
Appalachian Mountains	formed by the movement of Earth	plate collisions forced rocks to be formed

Show What You Know

1. C
2. C
3. volcanic activity
4. Answers will vary. Possible answers: The Great Plains have coal and other fossil fuels. The Canadian Shield contains rich minerals like silver, nickel, and gold.

Lesson Objectives

By the end of this lesson, your student will be able to:

- identify key natural resources found in North America
- describe how the use, distribution, and importance of natural resources can affect different groups
- identify the impact of trade on the availability of natural resources

Supporting Your Student

Explore
Engage your student in a discussion of where minerals like diamonds, gold, and nickel are found on Earth. As they explore the photo, ask them what they notice about the rock. Have a list of natural resources from your area ready to discuss. Think of opportunities where your student might have seen trading in real life (such as the grocery store, where you are trading money for the food you are buying).

Read (Use of Natural Resources)
Engage your student in a discussion about North America's food resources. It would be helpful to have them talk about what foods North America produces and why they are able to produce these foods. You might discuss what plants need to grow, like what type and amount of light each type of food requires, what the water requirements are, etc. You can look more closely at the hardiness zones map to determine which zones are best for which crops. You could explore crops that are typically grown in a single region, like cranberries.

Write (Renewable or Nonrenewable?)
Help your student to consider where the different types of natural resources come from. First, they all come from Earth, but where on Earth? For example, water sources come from rivers and oceans, but also from rain that fills those rivers and oceans. That rain renews the rivers and oceans. See if they can use this example to help them come up with additional examples.

Learning Styles

Auditory learners may enjoy listening to audio recordings of miners, both personal experiences and of actual mining taking place.

Visual learners may enjoy watching videos of mineral mining. They may enjoy watching the process of discovering gold, silver, or nickel.

Kinesthetic learners may enjoy exploring natural resources in their environment. It is best to research and choose an area where you know they might find something. They could look for things like water sources, plants, and animals.

Extension Activities

Create It
Have your student use the resources of their home, leftover things like paper towel rolls, old boxes, envelopes, and magazines, to create a painting, picture, or sculpture. Your student can use whatever materials they can find and create however they like. Allow them time to be creative and explore ways to use their resources.

Dig It Up
Have your student take some time to research places near their home that would be good for discovering natural resources. This might be a nearby park or forest, or perhaps you have an established business that allows for searching for natural resources. Engage in a discussion of the best method to search for natural resources (giving thought to taking care when digging, and then caring for what they find). If possible, and with permission from the site, travel to the site and participate in finding the natural resource.

Answer Key

Write *(What are some reasons that North America is able to produce a lot of the world's food?)*

Answers will vary. Possible answers: irrigation, a good climate for growing food, fertile soil, etc.

Write *(How would you define renewable and nonrenewable resources? What are some of their characteristics?)*

Answers will vary. Possible answers: All natural resources come from Earth. Renewable resources are all growing and living or can be replenished or refilled through natural processes. Nonrenewable resources are mined or have a limited supply.

Show What You Know

1. B
2. C
3. A
4. D
5. False
6. False
7. True
8. Answers will vary. Possible answers: coal, oil, nickel, silver, and agricultural, like grains
9. Answers will vary. Possible answers: Humans are using the natural resources, and in some cases, they are overusing them. As an example, factories and cars are using a lot more coal than in the past.

Lesson Objectives

By the end of this lesson, your student will be able to:

- describe the factors influencing human migration
- compare and contrast the factors leading to various mass migrations movements in North America
- identify the factors that led to the migration of people from one region in North America
- examine the influences and contributions of the migrants to the new region

Supporting Your Student

Take a Closer Look

Your student is given the opportunity to go to the library and check out a book that discusses what it is like to move to a new place. Some suggested titles are *The Name Jar* by Yangsook Choi, a story of a young girl who moves from Asia to North America and *Dreamers* by Yuyi Morales, a story of finding your way in a new place. In order to access these titles, you may search your local library or bookstore. In addition, if you use a search engine, you should find that both of these titles are available as read alouds online. Please read the titles before providing access to your student. As you read, notice that emotions play a large role in both of these stories. How can your student relate to the emotions in their own way?

Practice *(Factors of Migration)*

As your student explores the factors of migration, engage them in a discussion of what situations one might be in to be willing (or forced) to move to a new area. You can ask them guiding questions like, "Would it be hard for you to move across the country?" or "What would make you consider a move like that?" You should ask your student to discuss with you, in their own words, what each of the migration factors means.

Write *(Think about your family. If you moved somewhere new, what talents or knowledge would you bring with you? How would you share it with others?)*

As your student explores what their family might bring with them if they moved somewhere new, engage them in a discussion of exploring what their family likes to do. Here they may discuss different hobbies or activities their family enjoys. Guide them to any special family recipes or traditions you may have as a starting point for their writing.

Learning Styles

Auditory learners may enjoy listening to songs, poetry, and other work of the Harlem Renaissance to gain an understanding of the time.

Visual learners may enjoy looking at artwork or watching a video of people panning for gold.

Kinesthetic learners may enjoy the experience of a panning for gold experiment. Use an online search engine to search "panning for gold experiments" to obtain the instructions for setting up this activity.

Extension Activities

You've Got the Blues Too

Have your student research popular blues songs and music. Allow them to get a feel for the lyrics and topics of the songs. Engage them in a discussion of the importance of music as a way to express yourself and how this type of music was brought to the Harlem area as a result of migration. Have your student write their own blues song. It may be just a chorus or an entire song.

Map It Out

Using a map of the continent of North America, show your student the areas people migrated to and from. Ask your student to think about what factors make people move to certain areas. Have your student research the population of major cities like Los Angeles, New York, Toronto, Mexico City, or Atlanta. Have them identify the factors that would contribute to people moving to these cities.

Answer Key

Practice *(Factors of Migration)*

Type of Migration	What factors influence this type of migration?
economic migration	new job opportunities, more land
social migration	family, friends, better life styles
environmental migration	natural disasters, like floods, hurricanes, tornadoes
political migration	escaping war or famine

Write *(Think about your family. If you moved somewhere new, what talents or knowledge would you bring with you? How would you share it with others?)*

Answers will vary. Possible answers: musical talents, writing talents, artistic talents, language abilities

Practice *(Different Movements Similar Outcomes)*

Answers will vary depending on which migration movements they choose. Make sure your student includes details such as where the movements originated, how the movements began, and the reasons for the movements in the Venn diagram.

Show What You Know

1. Answers will vary. Possible answers: economic, political, environmental, and social

2. Answers will vary. Possible answer: Migrants bring with them new ideas, music, art, food, and stories.

3. Answers will vary. Possible answer: For both migrations, people were seeking a financial reward. In the Bracero Program there was an organized program where the migrants knew they would be getting paid, whereas in the Gold Rush the migrants were betting on striking it rich.

4. B

5. True

6. True

Lesson Objectives

By the end of this lesson, your student will be able to:

- identify the location of key cultural features and relate their significance
- relate how cultural features in a region influence population, the economy, government, and transportation

Supporting Your Student

Read *(Cultural Features)*

As your student explores the cultural features of North America, extend their learning by asking them to think of other features they may be familiar with in North America. For example, you might ask, "What other traditions do you know that are celebrated throughout North America?" They may be able to tell you about traditions like July 4, Thanksgiving in the United States or Canada, popular sporting events, or landmarks.

Read *(Behaviors in Culture)*

Some examples of cultural features are more abstract, like etiquette and practices. Help your student understand that these are typical behaviors of most people in the culture, but not necessarily something that every single person does. You might share that in the United States, men generally remove their hats during a country's national anthem or that it is common for people to pull over or stop walking while a funeral procession passes.

Read *(Impact of Cultural Features)*

Offer your student an example of an important cultural feature where you live. Ask them guiding questions to help them make real life connections like, "Does this feature attract visitors? Does it employ people?", "Do a lot of people live near this feature?", or "Does this feature affect the economy in the area?"

Learning Styles

Auditory learners may enjoy listening to stories of the people who built the cultural features in this lesson.

Visual learners may enjoy exploring images of other popular, famous, or historical features in North America.

Kinesthetic learners may enjoy replicating one of the cultural features mentioned in this lesson using play-dough or clay.

Extension Activities

Create a Poster

Have your student research a specific cultural feature listed in this lesson or one from their own culture. Have them research the location, the significance, and the influence it has had on the region it's located in. Then have them create a poster to show the important aspects of their cultural feature.

Virtual Field Trip

Have your student select the cultural feature from this lesson they are most interested in. Search online for a virtual field trip of this feature. Watch and discuss it together.

Answer Key

Show What You Know

1. Answers will vary. Possible answer: People like to live where there are jobs. A strong economy means more money in an area.

2. Answers will vary. Possible answer: Places with unique cultural features often have more visitors. People need ways to travel like airplanes. Places with lots of people need ports for shipping. Buses help move people safely around an area.

3. Answers will vary. Possible answer: Popular destinations lead to people spending money at local businesses in the area. Popular destinations create job opportunities.

4. Answers will vary. Possible answer: Sometimes there are laws about national languages or holidays. Rules are sometimes needed to preserve historical sites. If there are a lot of people in an area, they may need special laws to keep everyone safe.

5. Answers will vary. Possible answers:

Cultural Feature	Feature and Location	Why is it important?
	Chapultepec Castle in Mexico City, Mexico	It is the first castle in North America. It was used as a military academy in Mexico.
	Statue of Liberty, New York	It was a gift to America from France. It is a symbol of freedom and opportunity in America.

Lesson Objectives

By the end of this lesson, your student will be able to:

- investigate the cultural geography of North America
- explore broader influences of North American culture on individuals and civilizations around the world
- discover the lasting impact of North American culture on everyday aspects of modern day life

Supporting Your Student

Read (North America's Cultural Influence)

While reading this section, remind your student that the amendment process is the way that people can add additional amendments to the Constitution. Remind them that judicial review is the process of the judicial branch reviewing laws to make sure they are legal constitutionally. You might ask guiding questions like, "What does judicial mean? Does it refer to one of the three branches of the US government?"

Write (Name and describe two ways that North America has influenced the world.)

As your student explores the ways North America has influenced the world, review the definition of cultural geography with them. Ask them to name the factors that are included (use of natural resources, economy, religion, government, and other aspects of culture). Ask your student guiding questions like, "What is an example of people using available natural resources? How could this be influential?" and "What is an example of economic activity? How could this be influential?"

Practice

Ask your student for examples from their own life of influential fashion, sports, entertainment, media, or another topic in the lesson. Ask them if they think this example is also influential or popular elsewhere in the world, and why they think so. Support your student here by sharing with them a restaurant, pastime, or other aspect of your life that is important to you that may have come from another continent or location.

Learning Styles

Auditory learners may enjoy listening to popular North American pop songs that have been re-recorded in other languages for global audiences. The Beatles have several songs they recorded in German, for example.

Visual learners may enjoy watching baseball games played in North America versus in other countries. Ask them to pay close attention to any differences they notice in the environments.

Kinesthetic learners may enjoy researching and learning popular dances that originated in North America and spread to other countries.

Extension Activities

Rules of the Game

As your student learned, baseball is a favorite North American pastime. The rules of baseball have changed over time and may be different in other countries. Have your student research the rules and regulations of baseball and compare it to the rules of baseball in other countries like Japan or Venezuela. How do they compare? Your student can write a report, short essay, or decide on their own creative presentation to show their learning.

Influence in the Other Direction

Other countries have influenced North America too! Have your student research TV shows or characters for young people that originated in a different country and found popularity in North America.

Answer Key

Explore

Answers will vary based on their own personalities, feelings, and imaginations. Possible answers: I would feel relieved to find something I recognized. I would be hopeful that whoever was inside could help me.

Write *(Name and describe two ways that North America has influenced the world.)*

Answers will vary. Possible answers: government policies or ideas, news programs, magazines, television, architecture, internet

Practice

Answers will vary. Possible answers:

Influence	How has this influence made an impact on everyday life?
fashion	People all over the world wear clothes every day, and styles like jeans and t-shirts have become very popular all over the world.
sports	Baseball is a favorite pastime of North America, but other countries have also begun to enjoy baseball because of its influence. Boys in Venezuela grow up hoping to be professional players.
film	Hollywood is the world's oldest film industry, and films *Casablanca, E.T. the Extra-Terrestrial*, and *The Wizard of Oz* are iconic.
fast food	Fast food restaurants provide consistent food quickly for people's busy lives. McDonald's is so popular, it is the world's largest restaurant company.

Show What You Know

1. False
2. True
3. False
4. False
5. True
6. B
7. C
8. Answers will vary. Possible answer: The US Constitution has been a model for other countries because it clearly defines the systems of governments and the rights of the people. This is important because it clearly establishes a set of rules for the country. The ideas of judicial review and a process for amendments has been influential on other countries.
9. Answers will vary. Possible answer: Home building styles reflect the ways humans interact with available natural resources, the economy, and the region's climate.

Lesson Objectives

By the end of this lesson, your student will review the following big ideas from Chapter 5:

- You can use topographic and geopolitical maps to tell the story of North America. (Lesson 44)
- Indigenous people live throughout North America and use the resources they have access to. (Lesson 45)
- North America has different types of settlements, and people chose to settle in certain North American regions for various reasons. (Lesson 46)
- North America has important physical features, like rivers and lakes. (Lesson 47)
- The Great Flood of 1927 had a massive impact, and the Mississippi River and Tributaries Project was established by the Army Corps of Engineers to control flooding of the Mississippi River. (Lesson 48)
- Hawaii and the Appalachian Mountains were formed by physical processes, and various natural resources can be found in the eight regions of North America because of these physical processes. (Lesson 49)
- North America's natural resources include coal, nickel, oil, silver, and grains. (Lesson 50)
- Many factors cause people to move from one place to another, and migrants bring many ideas and talents to an area when they move to it. (Lesson 51)
- North America has many important cultural features, landmarks, and places of interest. (Lesson 52)
- North America's architecture, entertainment, and food have influence around the world. (Lesson 53)

Supporting Your Student

Write *(North American Cultural Features)*
Your student should be able to think of other cultural features that have made an influence on the world. If your student is struggling to remember, refer back to Lesson 53 and engage your student in a discussion of what cultural features are. After they recall the meaning of cultural features, refer to the lesson to discuss how the features influenced the world.

Practice *(Cause and Effect)*
As your student explores the cause and effect relationship of the events in North America, it would be best to relate cause and effect to concrete subjects they may be more familiar with. For example, you might engage them in a discussion of what might happen if you kick a rock with no shoes on. The cause would be kicking the rock, and the effect would be hurting your toe. After you provide them with this example, discuss the first example of what happened as a result of African Americans being faced with poor economic conditions and treatment.

Learning Styles

Auditory learners may enjoy listening to historical accounts of how North America has evolved over time.

Visual learners may enjoy creating a map that shows the geographical features, migration movements of the people, and/or the settlements of the Indigenous people.

Kinesthetic learners may enjoy engaging in visualizing vocabulary using their bodies. They may want to act out the vocabulary words to demonstrate their understanding of the words.

Extension Activities

Flash Card Fury

Provide your student with cards (index cards, sticky notes, etc.) and have them write the important geographical features, events, physical processes, cultural features, and other important concepts from the chapters on the cards. Ask your student to correctly sort what they write into categories. For example, if they write the formation of Hawaii, they should put that in a category of physical processes.

Virtual Field Trip

Allow your student to use the internet to search for a topic of interest from the chapters they read. Topics of interest might include: baseball in North America, the First Nations of Canada, or the Great Flood of 1927, but any topic that was discussed could also be included. Search for videos, historical photos, personal viewpoints, or articles. Have your student keep a journal of what they have learned about their topic of interest and share it with you when they are done.

Answer Key

Write *(What other cultural features of North America have made an impact on the world?)*
Answers will vary. Possible answers: well-known amusement park, fast food restaurants, baseball

Practice *(Vocabulary)*
Answers will vary but should show an understanding of the vocabulary words.

Practice *(Cause and Effect)*

	Cause	Effect
Great Migration	Many African Americans in the South were faced with poor economic conditions and racial discrimination.	Many African Americans moved North, bringing new talents and the Harlem Renaissance.
Baseball	American culture spreads around the world and becomes popular.	People in other countries decided to create professional baseball leagues and build stadiums so they could play baseball too. In Venezuela, young boys grow up dreaming of playing Major League Baseball.
The Great Flood of 1927	Unusually heavy rains began in 1926 and continued for months, causing the levees on the Mississippi River to break.	The Mississippi River and Tributaries Project was created by the 1928 Flood Control Act. The Army Corps of Engineers built levees and floodways to prevent it from happening again.
The Coastal Region's Influence on Human Settlement	The coastal plain and the coastal range provided access to water, the ability to grow crops and raise livestock, and the ability to trade with its harbors and access to rivers.	Humans created successful settlements in these regions by trading, fishing, and farming.

Practice *(Summarizing Information)*

Answers will vary. Possible answers: Indigenous people—some Indigenous peoples in Canada, the United States, and Mexico settled in the grassland prairies, areas of land with grasses and some pine trees. They could build houses out of the pine trees, hunt buffalo, and grow crops like corn, beans, and peppers. Deforestation—deforestation is when all of the trees are cut down in a large area. Deforestation destabilizes the ecosystem, increases air pollution, and contributes to flooding. The animals in that area lose their homes, and sometimes the people in that area lose their homes and must move.

Quick Review

Refer to the statement your student circled in the Show What You Know section to self-assess their knowledge of the chapter concepts. Then to assist in determining if your student is ready to take the assessment, consider:

- Having your student explain what natural resources are and list some natural resources that are found in North America.
- Having your student explain how North America has influenced countries across the world.

Chapter Assessment

Fill each blank with a word from the Word Bank.

Word Bank: topographic   red cedar   water
Tula Hidalgo   hills
Army Corps of Engineers

1. A _____ map shows the landforms and elevation of North America.

2. The Pacific Coast First Nations had access to _____ to build large homes.

3. The Toltec settled in _____, Mexico.

4. Humans often settled near _____.

5. The physical geography of the Canadian Shield can be described as having _____, rivers, lakes, and thin layers of soil.

6. The Mississippi River and Tributaries Project gave power to the _____ to control flooding on the Mississippi River.

7. What type of map is shown below?

A. physical

B. geopolitical

C. topographic

8. What is the importance of the Isthmus of Panama?

A. It separates North America and Asia.

B. It is a strip of land that separates North America and South America.

C. It is the first waterway to connect North America with Asia.

9. What did the Mayans create to store fresh water?

A. sinks

B. buckets

C. reservoirs

10. What did the Army Corps of Engineers do to control the flooding on the Mississippi River?

A. adopted a levees only policy

B. built taller bridges

C. built levees and floodways

D. widened the river

11. How do people respond to deforestation?

A. They are ok with it.

B. They monitor it with satellites and aerial imagery.

C. They don't pay attention to it.

12. What physical process contributed to the development of resources in Hawaii?

A. volcanic activity

B. erosion

C. plate movement

Discover! SOCIAL STUDIES · GRADE 5 · CHAPTER 5 ASSESSMENT

143

13. How have humans affected the supply and quality of natural resources? Select all that apply.

    A. They have not affected the supply.

    B. They use the resources and replace them if they are renewable.

    C. They use the resources, but sometimes to excess.

14. Why is it important for people who build in Canada to have homes that can withstand the climate?

    A. The hot, desert-like summers require good ventilation systems.

    B. The cold winters cause a lot of freezing and thawing, and the buildings need to be able to withstand the temperature changes.

    C. The people don't want to be hot.

Match the type of settlement with the picture.

15.

_____

16.

_____

17.

_____

18.

_____

    A. village

    B. city

    C. hamlet

    D. town

19. True or False   Coal is a natural resource found in North America.

20. True or False   Oil is used in making cosmetics.

21. Look at the cultural feature pictured below and describe its significance.

Cultural Feature	Why is it important?

22. Compare and contrast the Bracero Program to the Gold Rush.

....

....

....

....

23. Describe how the resources of the Basin and Range differ from those found on the Rocky Mountains.

....

....

....

....

24. Explain and describe the factors that lead to human migration. Provide one example of human migration in North America.

....

....

....

....

25. Describe how the media makes an impact worldwide.

....

....

....

....

Chapter Assessment Answer Key

1. topographic
2. red cedar
3. Tula, Hidalgo
4. water
5. hills
6. Army Corps of Engineers
7. B
8. B
9. C
10. C
11. B
12. A
13. B, C
14. B
15. city
16. town
17. village
18. hamlet
19. True
20. True

22. Answers will vary. Possible answer: The Bracero Program was initiated by the government and was intended for people who were in search of work. The Gold Rush was a discovery and anyone who could find transportation could get to California. Both caused economic migration.

23. Answers will vary. Possible answers: the lumber available in the mountains along with coal; copper, zinc, and other minerals available in the basin and range

24. Answers will vary. Possible answers: social, economic, environmental, or political; examples include the Gold Rush, Great Migration, or Bracero Program

25. Answers will vary. Possible answers: The media, such as radio and television, reaches listeners and viewers worldwide. Many people from other countries enjoy watching the media because it presents an idea of average life across North America.

21. Answers will vary. Possible answers:

Cultural Feature	Why is it important?
	This is Mt. Rushmore in South Dakota, and it is important because it has four of the United States presidents carved into the mountainside.
	This is the White House in Washington, DC, in the United States. It is important because it is the center of government for the country. It is where the US president lives.

146

Discover! SOCIAL STUDIES • GRADE 5 • CHAPTER 5 ASSESSMENT

Alternative Assessment

Project: Poster

For this project, you will create a poster with a map of North America and label it with various physical and cultural features you learned about in the chapter.

Project Requirements or Steps:

1. Find a map of North America. This may be a geopolitical, topographic, or tourist map.

2. Label at least two physical features of North America.

3. Identify why the two physical features of North America are significant and at least one impact each physical feature has had on human settlements or migration.

4. Label at least four cultural features of North America.

5. Identify why the four cultural features of North America are significant.

6. Share your poster with friends and family.

Alternative Assessment Rubric

Use the following rubric to grade your student's assessment.

	4	3	2	1	Points
Connection to the Chapter	The project is clearly connected to the chapter.	The project is connected to the chapter.	The project is somewhat connected to the chapter.	The project is not connected to the chapter.	
Creativity	The project is very creative and aesthetically appealing.	The project is creative and aesthetically appealing.	The project is somewhat creative and aesthetically appealing.	The project is not creative or aesthetically appealing.	
Information	The information or data is very accurate and easy to follow.	The information or data is accurate.	The information or data is somewhat accurate.	The information or data is not accurate.	
Grammar and Mechanics	There are no grammar and punctuation mistakes.	There are one or two grammar and punctuation mistakes.	There are several grammar and punctuation mistakes.	There are a distracting number of grammar and punctuation mistakes.	

Total Points _____/16

Average _____

148

Discover! SOCIAL STUDIES • GRADE 5 • CHAPTER 5 ASSESSMENT

Lesson Objectives

By the end of this lesson, your student will be able to:

- examine different maps of South America
- determine what story each map tells
- compare and contrast the major cities in South America and the cities in your state/country

Supporting Your Student

Explore

For this activity, ask your student to brainstorm areas they have visited. Does your student have pictures that may help them remember a destination they have visited? Allow your student to use a search engine to look up pictures from the city, state, or country they visited as a refresher.

Read *(Maps of South America)*

Remind your student you will need maps in many different situations. Maybe a biologist is studying animals that live in high elevations. Which map would this scenario apply to? They might use a topographic map. Maybe a historian is studying a city of interest, and they need to visit the city to conduct research at local museums. They might use a tourist map. What if a traveler is setting a goal of visiting each country on the continent or each city in a country? They might use a geopolitical map. Maybe a historian wants to study how country boundaries have changed over the years. They might use a geopolitical map.

Read *(Every Map Tells a Story)*

As your student is reading about the different major cities in South America, ask them to highlight characteristics that are similar to their own city in one color. Ask your student to highlight characteristics that are different from their own city in another color. This will also help them choose the city to use in the assessment short-answer question.

Learning Styles

Auditory learners may enjoy listening to a podcast about South America. Here are topics you can search on the internet to find an appropriate podcast:

1. *podcast on South America for kids*
2. *podcast on major cities in South America for kids*

Visual learners may enjoy coloring and labeling an outline map of South America. Use the internet and type *outline map of South America*. Print the map. Allow your student to color the countries and label them. Your student can refer to the maps provided throughout the lesson. If your student wants to sketch the map, this is also an option.

Kinesthetic learners may enjoy acting as a compass. Your student can use a labeled map from the lesson and travel north to northern countries. Your student can travel south and narrate which southern country they are visiting. Your student can travel east and narrate which eastern country they are visiting. Your student can travel west and narrate which western country they are visiting in South America.

Extension Activities

South America's Country Flags

Have your student create a book of flags for each country in South America. Your student can use index cards for this. Gather 14 index cards. Have your student write the name of each country on the front and then research the flag for the country. Your student can draw a picture of the flag on the back. Then quiz your student by holding up the flag for the country to see if your student can name the corresponding country.

Travel Brochure

Your student will choose three major cities of interest from the cities described. Your student will create a trifold travel brochure. The cover should show South America and have a creative title. The inside of the brochure should have each city described in a single folded area. Your student could print a map or pictures of important destinations within each section as well.

Answer Key

Show What You Know

1. geopolitical
2. topographic
3. tourist
4. B, D
5. A
6. A

Geographic Factors and Human Settlement in South America

Lesson Objectives

By the end of this lesson, your student will be able to:

- analyze geographic factors that influence where people live and how people came to settle South America
- develop spatial understanding of the location of geographic features in South America compared with those studied in previous chapters
- identify geographic connections between the continents

Supporting Your Student

Create

It takes a fair amount of abstract thinking to imagine what life would be like without a specific landform or geographic feature. Support your student by asking guiding questions like, "What do (mountains/lakes/ rivers/etc.) provide for people, animals, and plants?," "What do you like about (their chosen landform)?," "What would the area look like without it?," and "How would this impact the available resources in the area?" Because their short story is a work of fiction, it is okay (encouraged, even!) for your student to be creative and fantastical with their writing—the focus should be more on the engagement with the idea than the accuracy of their predictions.

Explore

Help inspire your student's creative vision by showing them examples of other quadriptych works of art. Your student can simply imagine the landscape they have chosen, or you can go to that particular landscape to sketch in nature. If you have specific memories of the location during different seasons, share those memories and observations with your student to help them plan their work of art.

Learning Styles

Auditory learners may enjoy reading aloud a passage about the Amazon Rain Forest. Use a search engine to search 'reading passages on the Amazon rainforest'. Allow your student to read the passage aloud to you. When your student is done, ask your student some new things they learned about the rain forest.

Visual learners may enjoy drawing a picture of each of the geographic features. Your student can fold a paper into fourths and in each box should draw an example of a geographic feature found in South America.

Kinesthetic learners may enjoy acting out each geographic feature. Your student can pretend they are climbing up a mountain, and you should guess "Andes Mountains." You could act out rowing a canoe down a river, and your student should guess "Amazon River."

Extension Activities

Geographic Feature Posters

Your student can research four specific examples of geographic features throughout South America to create a series of educational posters displaying the feature artistically and listing important facts about the feature.

Book of ABCs

Your student can create a book of ABCs on South America. They will need 26 index cards or pieces of paper. Hole punch the index cards and tie them together with a piece of yarn. Allow your student to find facts about South America or places in South America that begin with each letter of the alphabet.

Answer Key

Write *(If you were an early human settler, which geographic feature would you choose to settle near and why?)*

Answers will vary. Possible answer: I would choose the Andes Mountains. There is fertile soil to grow crops and the glaciers provide a fresh water source.

Show What You Know

1. B
2. A, C
3. False
4. Indigenous people moved south from North and Central America into South America.
5. The Amazon River system was expansive. It provided a source of travel, trade, and fish. Indigenous people could move further into the forest for protection. Rainfall helped to supply water.

Lesson Objectives

By the end of this lesson, your student will be able to:

- examine evidence of common patterns and features of human settlements
- compare and contrast human settlements of different regions in South America
- analyze how the environment influenced the settlements

Supporting Your Student

In the Real World

As you discuss your student's choices with them, you may find they don't necessarily know what the most useful tools for survival might be. Be sure to have them thoroughly explain their choices and what they would use each item for. You might also ask guiding questions like, "Did you know you could use the mirror or aluminum foil to signal with, since they are reflective?" or "What would you do for food once you finished the beans?"

Explore

If your student has never camped before, consider using the internet to find a video of what it is like to go camping. Look up pictures of mountains, lakes, and oceans and see if your student can identify items that are already there that might help with survival. Ask your students what items are missing that will be needed.

Read (Environment and Settlements)

Your student can use two different color highlighters to annotate the information in the table visually by marking characteristics that would make settlement easy and characteristics that would make settlement more difficult. Once they complete the table, discuss their answers together.

Learning Styles

Auditory learners may enjoy writing a poem about each region. Your student can choose words from each region that are easy to rhyme. Ask your student to create a short poem with hints about the characteristics in each region and read it aloud.

Visual learners may enjoy researching the traditional home building styles in each region of South America and viewing images of different areas and their architecture.

Kinesthetic learners may enjoy acting as a compass. Review the cardinal directions of a compass (north, south, east, and west). Allow the student to practice the moves for each direction. As you provide a hint or characteristic that corresponds with a particular region of South America, the student should travel in the direction of the region.

Extension Activities

Four Square

Have your student fold a sheet of paper into fourths. Each section should be labeled with a particular South American region. Your student can make a collage of pictures that associate with the descriptive patterns provided for the region. Your student should color the pictures so it is attractive.

Climate Study

Have your student choose one country from each region and record the weather in that location each day for a week. Be sure your student notes the city and country they are recording. At the end of the week, have your student examine the data to see if they are reflective of what they have learned about the climate zones in South America.

Answer Key

Show What You Know

1. A, C
2. Incas
3. False
4. Answers will vary. Possible answers: If the climate is cold, humans will have difficulty remaining warm and safe in colder weather. If the climate is too dry, humans will struggle accessing water for themselves, agriculture, and animals. If there is too much rain, homes and crops could be washed away.

Physical Geography and Natural Resources of South America

Lesson Objectives

By the end of this lesson, your student will be able to:

- investigate the physical geography of South America
- analyze the influence of the effects of people's relationship to natural resources on the development of various Indigenous South American civilizations

Supporting Your Student

Explore
Help your student consider different options for transporting water, like bucket brigades or pulleys. You can also discuss digging wells and irrigation methods that might be useful.

Read (*Physical Geography of South America*)
It can be challenging to visualize environments we've never seen before. You might support your student by showing them images of the different regions in South America to help them picture them mentally. Visualization is a key skill for comprehension and retention of information.

Practice
Support your student in completing the table by asking guiding questions like, "Have you used water today? How did you use it?" and "What can be made out of clay? What were those things good for?"

Learning Styles

Auditory learners may enjoy listening to an interview by present-day Inca about their culture. Use a search engine to find podcasts and interviews with Incas.

Visual learners may enjoy drawing pictures of items or homes that Indigenous people of South American used or lived in. Use a search engine to look for information about the lives of Indigenous people of South America. Let your student choose the image that speaks to them the most. Your student should include a caption of how the item relates to South America.

Kinesthetic learners may enjoy making a model canoe or home that replicates the canoes or homes used by the Indigenous people of South America.

Extension Activities

Potato-Potahto
Inspired by your student's online connection activity, have them prepare a traditional Peruvian potato recipe together. There are many to choose from available online, including papas a la huancaina and papas rellenas.

Llamas, Alpacas, and Vicunas, Oh My!
Have your student watch video(s) about the importance of alpacas, llamas, vicunas, and other similar animals in the Andes. Your student can create a slideshow or poster about the uses for these animals and how they are cared for by Andean shepherds.

Physical Geography and Natural Resources of South America

Answer Key

Practice

Answers will vary. Possible answers:

Natural Resource	What would life have been like without this natural resource?
Water	Without water, Indigenous people would not be able to survive. They needed fresh water to drink and the water was where fish lived. They ate fish.
Trees	Trees helped the indigenous people greatly with their homes, canoes, weapons, and tools. They would lack all of these items without trees, which would make life very difficult. They would not have been able to live in the rainforest without trees as a resource.
Fish	Without fish, Indigenous people would have less food to eat, which would make it harder to live.
Fruits	Indigenous people would be more malnourished without all of the fruits. They also would not have as much to trade with others.
Clay	Indigenous people would have a harder time containing their foods or cooking their foods. They would also have fewer ways of producing art. Clay helped to keep homes warm, as well.
Stone	Without stone, the Incas would not have become the massive empire that they were. They would not have been able to build roads and cities.

Show What You Know

1. C
2. C
3. True
4. Answers will vary. Possible answers: water, trees, fish, fruits, clay, stone
5. Answers will vary. Possible answers: They would lack canoes, homes, utensils, and weapons, such as bows and arrows. Leaves and bark were used for roofs.

Lesson Objectives

By the end of this lesson, your student will be able to:

- explain how people make and respond to changes in their environment in various ways
- identify the significance of the Inca road system
- examine other ways that people in South America made changes to their environment
- illustrate examples of how they responded to changes in the environment

Supporting Your Student

Play

Observe your student as they construct their earthen landform. Allow them to troubleshoot without intervention as they try to affect the landform with air and water. If they need suggestions, you might offer advice like, "Try pouring the water a little more slowly and evenly" or "See what happens when you create a channel for the water to flow through."

Explore

Your student may or may not have a keen sense of direction when it comes to the roads in your community. Gauge their awareness by having them give directions to the listed locations aloud. As they list alternative routes, you might offer insights they don't think of. This might sound like, "But remember, that road dead ends before Main Street" or "Does that street cross over the Waterville River?"

Read (South America's Environmental Changes)

As your student reads about erosion and sediment, ask them to recall and describe how their mud/sand/gravel/etc. moved with the flow of water. Ask, "Where did your sediment go? What happened to the land where the water flowed?"

Read (Adapting to Changes)

As your student considers the ways glacial melting could impact human life in the region, ask them to visualize and imagine being in this situation. Ask your student how they might respond to this challenge or to propose alternative opportunities for the people who rely on glacial water and the economic opportunities tourism brings to the area.

Learning Styles

Auditory learners may enjoy listening to a podcast about efforts by advocates and conservationists working to preserve the Amazon Rainforest.

Visual learners may enjoy painting a landscape inspired by the geographic regions and features of South America.

Kinesthetic learners may enjoy delivering a message chaski-style! Allow your student to play runner and deliver a message to a friend or family member nearby. Have them recruit others to assist in the message-carrying if possible.

Extension Activities

Modeling Plate Tectonics

Have your student search online for "graham cracker plate tectonics" experiments. Using some simple food ingredients, your student can see first-hand how the movement of the lithosphere affects landforms—and they might even end up with a tasty snack!

Conserving the Amazon

Your student can email conservation groups or conservationists working in the field to learn more about what kids and families can do from afar to support their work of preserving the Amazon Rainforest. They can even extend the conversation into an interview and share it by submitting it to a local publication or producing a podcast.

Adapting to Changes in the Environment in South America

Answer Key

1. 3

2. 2

3. 1

4. 4

5. roads

6. communication

7. chaskis

8. Common people

9. government

10. Answers will vary. Possible answers: If they have to move if water is unavailable, it can hurt economic opportunity and the availability of fish. They may have to adapt their agricultural practices by digging wells, developing irrigation methods, or collecting rainwater.

11. Answers will vary. Possible answers: People are equipping others with tools and supplies to fight forest fires. They are also offering education about sustainable forestry and fire-safe development.

Lesson Objectives

By the end of this lesson, your student will be able to:

- identify the physical processes that contribute to the availability and abundance of a natural resource
- compare and contrast the availability and distribution of natural resources in South America across regions

Supporting Your Student

Create

Encourage your student to add what they know about the water cycle to a diagram. If they do not remember specific vocabulary, encourage them to show what they know in pictures. When they are finished, work together to add vocabulary such as evaporation, water vapor, condensation, precipitation, and collection to the diagram. Find other visual models online together and use them to add more to your student's diagram.

Explore

Remind your student that the water cycle is a natural process. It changes the earth in some way and provides a natural resource. Ask your student to think of another natural resource (i.e., rock, vegetables, wind) and how it is created. Ask your student what they know about what this resource needs. Through this prompting, you can lead them to discover another natural process. Natural disasters are natural processes too. Discussing the outcome or effect of a natural disaster such as a wildfire, hurricane, or blizzard, can provide your student with understanding of this concept.

Read (South America's Natural Resources)

Help your student compare and contrast the regions of South America by prompting the use of compare and contrast vocabulary. *While, but, however, similarly, different,* and *although* are all great compare and contrast words. These can be written on cards for use when speaking or writing. Looking up a map of South America's natural resources online is another great way to provide a resource to help your student

compare and contrast the different regions in South America and their resources.

Learning Styles

Auditory learners may enjoy recording a description of the Amazon, Pampas, and Coastal regions of South America. Then they can listen to their recordings as a review of the material.

Visual learners may enjoy finding different maps of South America's resources online.

Kinesthetic learners may enjoy turning the continent of South America into a jigsaw puzzle. Print a blank copy of the continent. Have your student draw or write natural resources found in the different regions, and then cut the continent into pieces. Have your student practice putting the pieces together.

Extension Activities

Make a Resource Map

Print out a blank outline of South America. Have your student outline the main geographical regions such as the Amazon Basin, Pampas region, Andes Mountains, Coastal region, and Atacama Desert or countries. Add symbols to represent different resources found in each country or region.

Natural Processes Diagram

If your student has a love of science, give them the opportunity to research more natural processes. Have your student create a diagram showing the series of steps in the process they chose. Have your student list the natural resources affected or created during this process.

Answer Key

Explore
Answers will vary. Possible answers: Pollination helps plants reproduce. Photosynthesis helps plants create energy to survive.

Take a Closer Look
Answers will vary. Possible answers: I see mountains and areas of dry land. Maybe I see a desert! Because I see the Amazon Rainforest, I know there is wood, but there may also be other plants or animals people can use as a resource.

Write (How are natural resources created?)
Answers will vary. Possible answer: Natural resources are created through natural processes. For example, soil is created when rocks are worn down through erosion. Plants are able to grow when the hydrologic and climatic processes provide water.

Write (What do you notice about the availability of resources in the country of Brazil?)
Answers will vary. Possible answer: Brazil has an abundance of many different resources while other countries have fewer resources due to their geographical location and climate.

Practice
1. Resources found in the Amazon Rainforest: fresh water, lumber, tropical fruits, metals
2. Resources found in Pampas region: soil, agricultural resources such as corn, wheat, and livestock
3. Resource found in the Andes: copper
4. Resource found in the Coastal regions of Peru and Chile: fish
5. Resources found in Brazil: lumber, petroleum, tropical fruits, nuts, iron, and gold
6. Resource found in Venezuela: petroleum

Show What You Know
1. C
2. B
3. Copper Ore
4. Answers will vary. Possible answers: The climate affects natural resources because temperature and precipitation impact which plants and animals can survive in an area.

Online Connection
Answers will vary. Possible answers: In an ocean food web, different types of fish are natural resources that result from the natural process.

Importance of Natural Resources in South America

Lesson Objectives

By the end of this lesson, your student will be able to:

- identify key natural resources found in South America
- describe how the use, distribution, and importance of natural resources can affect different groups.
- identify the impact of trade on the availability of natural resources

Supporting Your Student

Explore

When asking your student to draw a conclusion, prompt them by asking them to think about their background information. What did they learn in the previous chapter that could help them draw a conclusion? Encourage them to use the resources from the memory game as clues as well.

Read (Agriculture in South America)

You can model the difference between a surplus and a deficit with two cups and ice. Fill one cup with ice until it is filled completely or overflowing. Keep your cup empty. Ask your student which cup has a surplus and which has a deficit. Ask if they can spare any ice from the overflowing cup. If so, they have a surplus.

Take a Closer Look (Amazon Rainforest)

Remind your student that to make a judgment about this situation, they need to consider all of the groups affected. Ask your student to explain why groups might feel they need to destroy parts of the Amazon. Ask your student to explain why Indigenous tribes should remain in the Amazon. Encourage your student to support their thinking using these details.

Learning Styles

Auditory learners may enjoy alternating reading paragraphs aloud with the instructor giving them the opportunity to listen. They may also enjoy having a debate about an important issue from the text.

Visual learners may enjoy drawing pictures to accompany or replace answers to questions.

Kinesthetic learners may enjoy using movement to answer yes or no questions. Your student chooses a movement that means *yes* and another that means *no*. The instructor can review information from the text allowing the student to respond using their chosen movements.

Extension Activities

Resource Hunt

Help your student find as many products from South America as they can in your local grocery store. Have them take a picture of each resource they find. Visit another store and see if they can find more South American products!

Indigenous Tribe Research

Have your student research one or more Indigenous tribes from the Amazon. Then have them write a report or create a poster providing information in the following sections: tribe name, language, population, resources they use, and beliefs. They can add pictures or photos to their project.

Answer Key

Explore
Answers will vary. Possible answer: I think South America sells lumber to other countries because there are so many trees in the Amazon.

Write *(How does agriculture differ across the continent of South America?)*
Each region grows different resources. The Amazon and Pampas grow a surplus of goods. Bananas and coffee are grown in the Amazon. Wheat and corn are grown in the Pampas region.

Practice

Cause	Effect
A surplus of coffee, bananas, and iron are grown or mined in Brazil.	Coffee, bananas, and iron are traded with other nations.
There is a high demand for beef.	Ranchers burn parts of the Amazon Rainforest to make room for more cattle ranches.
Answers will vary. Possible answer: Tropical fruits grown in the Amazon are in demand.	Indigenous tribes are forced off their lands.
Large quantities of trees grow in the Amazon.	Lumber is exported to other nations.
Jobs in cities and jobs mining for valuable metals pay higher wages.	Farmers and workers may move into cities or near mines.

Show What You Know
1. A
2. True
3. Indigenous
4. deficit
5. Answers will vary. Possible answer: There are more services available in cities.

Lesson Objectives

By the end of this lesson, your student will be able to:

- extend understanding that human migration is influenced by many factors and that people migrate for voluntary and involuntary reasons
- compare and contrast the factors contributing to various mass migrations to Brazil
- identify the factors that led to the migration of people from one region in South America
- examine the influences and contributions of the migrants to the new region

Supporting Your Student

Play

Your student may need assistance holding the pencil or flicking their paper clip to use their rudimentary spinner. Have your student practice making and using the spinner a few times before they complete their final spin.

After selecting their country and completing the activities that follow, spinning again and discussing how immigrating to another country would be different, could provide the opportunity for valuable learning.

Explore

Encourage your student to think about previous lessons focusing on the climate, physical features, and resources of South America. They can use this information and further research to help them decide what to bring to their new home. Is the climate tropical? Ask your student what type of clothes they will need. What type of work might they do there? Are there agricultural resources that might lead to a career in farming? This might mean your student is going to bring a book about growing coffee beans!

Read (Immigrants in Brazil)

Discuss the meaning of *diversity* to help build understanding. Is your student's community diverse? Ask them how to decide. Tell your student that *diversity* can mean people in a community have different beliefs, abilities, ethnic backgrounds, educational levels, or resources. What can one learn from members of a diverse community?

Take a Closer Look (Natural Disasters Cause Involuntary Immigration)

Find Haiti on a map. Explain that Haiti is a country in North America, part of the Caribbean Islands. Earthquakes are common in this area. Ask your student for other examples of natural disasters and why natural disasters can make migration involuntary.

Learning Styles

Auditory learners may enjoy listening to immigrant stories. Many podcasts are dedicated to sharing stories of immigration. Find one to listen to for a week.

Visual learners may enjoy reading the worktext with a world map at hand. Countries and continents can be found for review.

Kinesthetic learners may enjoy mapping the different immigration routes that have been taken to Brazil. Encourage your student to label each route or provide a color key.

Extension Activities

Immigration Museum Exploration

Have your student visit the website for the Immigration Museum of the State of São Paulo. Have them view the online exhibits and record questions that come to mind as they look at the photographs of different immigrant experiences. Have them choose two or three questions to research and answer with you.

Immigrant Biography

Have your student research and write about Andreas Pavel. Born in Germany, Pavel immigrated to Brazil at age six. Pavel became an inventor. He is credited with inventing the Walkman, or personal stereo. Encourage your student to draw conclusions about the contributions and innovation immigrants can bring to their new countries.

Answer Key

Play
Answers will vary. Possible answers: Brazil, Portuguese, corn, beef, tropical fruits, city of São Paulo, lumber, tropical fruits and nuts

Explore
Answers will vary. Possible answers: rain jacket, hiking shoes, light clothing, passport, sunscreen

Write *(What is the difference between voluntary and involuntary immigration?)*
Answers will vary. Possible answers: Voluntary immigration or migration is when people want to move to a new country but do not need to move. Involuntary immigration or migration is when people must move to survive.

Practice

Voluntary	Involuntary
job	war
education	oppression
family	natural disaster

Write *(Why do people migrate to Brazil from other South American countries?)*
Answers will vary. Possible answers: People migrate to Brazil from other countries in South America because there are more opportunities to work. In some countries, such as Venezuela, lack of resources leads people to migrate to Brazil.

Write *(Why do people migrate from the Andes region to the Amazon region of Brazil?)*
Japanese immigrants migrated to Brazil when the US military took control of land on the island of Okinawa.

Show What You Know
1. D, E
2. Answers will vary. Possible answer: They provide labor, skills, and culture that improve the society.
3. False
4. Venezuela

Lesson Objectives

By the end of this lesson, your student will be able to:

- identify cultural features found in South America
- describe how cultural features in a region of South America influence factors of daily life, such as the economy, government, or transportation

Supporting Your Student

Explore

Your student has learned an incredible amount about world geography so far. Some of the finer points may have gotten fuzzy over the weeks and months since they've studied some of the earlier topics. Refresh their memory by asking guiding questions like, "What cultural features do you remember from Asia (or Africa, Europe, etc.)?," "How did (this cultural feature) impact daily life?," and "In what ways can (art/dress/language/public works/etc.) have a larger influence on people's day-to-day lives?"

Read (Cultural Expression)

For context, it might be helpful to your student to review the other cultural features lessons briefly to remember what cultural features are, which ones they have learned about previously, and how they relate to and influence daily life. Discussing the dress of all South American peoples could be its own chapter! It might be helpful for your student to view images of traditional and typical ways of dressing in the different regions of South America to provide additional context (and provide additional scaffolding for highly visual learners).

Learning Styles

Auditory learners may enjoy listening to interviews or podcasts that include people from South America talking about the ways they express their culture.

Visual learners may enjoy locating the features in the lesson on a map or even creating their own!

Kinesthetic learners may enjoy creating a model of a South American cultural feature from clay or building it out of interconnecting building blocks or other craft supplies.

Extension Activities

Virtual Tourist

Your student can take a virtual field trip of one (or more) of the cultural features discussed in the lesson. Once they are done, they can create a slideshow presentation of photos of and around the cultural feature and pretend they are sharing photos of their trip while also sharing what they learned.

DIY Dress

Your student can further research traditional dress throughout South America and select a garment or accessory to make themselves. This could be an article of clothing, jewelry, bag/purse, hat, or whatever they discover that strikes their interest.

Answer Key

Explore
Answers will vary depending on what region of the world your student chooses. Possible answers: Sports and activities like baseball can spread to other countries and continents, people all over the world watch films made in Hollywood, monuments like the Eiffel Tower or Great Wall of China attract lots of tourists, which can benefit the local economy, popular tourist destinations create traffic problems that need to be addressed, etc.

For the second part, their answer will be a prediction, so it's not about getting it right or wrong. Review and discuss their response to make sure their thought process is well-reasoned.

Write (How do you think the presence of so many cultures for so many years has influenced the religious tolerance of South America?)
South America is very diverse with people from all different backgrounds and cultures. Accepting their religious expression makes South America a welcoming place.

Practice
Answers will vary. Possible answer:

Christ the Redeemer Statue: This is such a popular tourist attraction that structures had to be built in order to allow people to access it, like the stairs in the picture. They probably needed to build roads and a place to park too.

Casa Grande del Pueblo: This is a new, exciting building. Since people want to tour it, but important government officials are also present, they probably need a lot of security in the area.

Show What You Know
1. I
2. E
3. D
4. H
5. G
6. J
7. C
8. A
9. F
10. B
11. government
12. economic
13. transportation
14. population
15. government
16. transportation

Lesson Objectives

By the end of this lesson, your student will be able to:

- investigate the cultural geography of South America
- explore influences of South American culture on individuals and civilizations around the world
- discover the impact of South American culture on everyday aspects of life

Supporting Your Student

Take a Closer Look

Support your student by helping them locate different types of ballpoint pens to examine stick pens, push-button retraction, and twist retraction. This way, they can see different designs and explore each component of how they work. This is an excellent exercise in understanding how something so simple that we often take for granted is usually due to lots of design, engineering, and revision.

Explore

If your student has difficulty thinking of ways that cultural exchange has happened coming into their country and back out again, provide relevant examples that will jog their memory, or do additional research. You might suggest examples of arts and culture groups that an immigrant community has developed or examples of restaurants that share and exchange culture through food in the community.

Write (How do famous singers or sports stars promote cultural diplomacy around the world?)

Ask your student to think through the question in order to best develop their answer. Ask guiding questions like, "What do entertainers and athletes do for their work?," "How does their work contribute to the culture of their country and the world?," and "What do people think about entertainers and athletes?"

Learning Styles

Auditory learners may enjoy listening to the music of South American musicians, like Juanes or Pery Ribeiro.

Visual learners may enjoy examining different kinds of wool-weaving from various regions of South America.

Kinesthetic learners may enjoy learning some *samba* dance moves!

Extension Activities

Invention Investigation

Your student can research other inventions that originated from South America and how those inventions have impacted the world. They can present their findings in a digital slideshow presentation.

Up Close and Personal

Your student can research *samba* dance or music groups in their local community. If there are any, attend a performance to learn more about this important cultural art form! If there are not any samba groups, look for other South American cultural groups or events that you could attend.

Answer Key

Write *(What is one difference cultural geography and cultural diplomacy make in the world?)*

Answers will vary. Possible answer: Cultural diplomacy helps people appreciate and respect different cultures, which can create goodwill and good relationships between countries.

Write *(How do famous singers or sports stars promote cultural diplomacy around the world?)*

Answers will vary. Possible answer: Entertainers and athletes share their talent with the world and represent their country while doing it. This helps to create a positive feeling toward their culture or country.

Show What You Know

1. geography
2. samba
3. Andes Mountains
4. wood
5. exports
6. diplomacy
7. heart
8. Answers will vary. Possible answer: Cultural exchange allows people to express the culture and share it with others, which helps people outside the culture understand it better.
9. Answers will vary. Possible answer: The ruins of ancient societies throughout the Andes attract a lot of visitors each year, which promotes curiosity about history and other cultures. When people visit these places today, they also learn about the culture there now.

Lesson Objectives

By the end of this lesson, your student will review the following big ideas from Chapter 6, "South America."

- Maps can tell stories about South America's land and its features. (Lesson 55)
- Landforms and geographic features impact where and how humans settled across South America. (Lesson 56)
- Human settlement is influenced by the environment and its changes. (Lesson 57)
- Indigenous peoples of South America built advanced societies that made use of available resources in ways that influenced humans that settled later. (Lesson 58)
- Environments change over time, both through natural processes and by human change. (Lesson 59)
- South America is rich with natural resources because of the vastly different environmental regions, like the Andes Mountains, Amazon River, and Amazon Rainforest. (Lesson 60)
- Timber from the dense forests across South America is one of the continent's greatest resources, along with metals, wool, petroleum, and agriculture. (Lesson 61)
- People migrate to other countries for voluntary and involuntary reasons. (Lesson 62)
- South America is made up of many different cultures, and human migration has led to a lot of cultural exchange influencing those cultures. (Lesson 63)
- Because South America has a long history of cultural exchange through human migration, complex cultures have developed throughout South America. (Lesson 64)

Supporting Your Student

Create
Help your student brainstorm ideas for ways to illustrate or visually represent each big idea. Ask guiding questions like, "What could you draw to represent the exchange of culture?" and "What

image would represent the idea of abundant natural resources?" You can also look for different quilt patterns if your student would like to do something more adventurous than a basic grid.

Review (Maps)
South America has many geographic features, and your student has learned about many of them. You can support your student by asking them to name examples of certain types of geographic features from the chapter, like rivers, lakes, forests, etc.

Review (Indigenous Resources, Culture, and Influence)
Ask your student to narrate to you what they have learned about South American culture by giving examples. If they have difficulty getting started, ask them a guiding question like, "What did you learn about music and dance as it relates to culture in South America?" and "How does dress reflect culture in South America?"

Learning Styles

Auditory learners may enjoy completing the vocabulary activity orally.

Visual learners may enjoy creating a collage that expresses the big ideas of the chapter.

Kinesthetic learners may enjoy sculpting the landforms and geographic features of South America out of air-dry clay.

Extension Activities

Tourism Commercial
Your student can create a travel and tourism advertisement video exploring the cultures and features of South America. Direct your student to use plenty of engaging visuals and to promote features that are good examples of what they learned in this chapter.

Culinary Tour
Your student can research foods from different regions across South America. Have your student design and plan a menu for a feast that represents each region. If possible, prepare the feast with your

student and discuss the exciting dishes and flavors you experience!

Answer Key

Review (Maps)

Answers will vary. Possible answers:

Andes Mountains: fresh water from glaciers, good place to raise animals like alpacas and llamas

Patagonian Desert: great place for raising animals like horses and sheep, runoff from the Andes collects in freshwater lakes

Amazon River: massive waterway that provides fish and a way to travel long distances, opportunities for trade, fresh water

Amazon Rainforest: abundant timber, diverse plant and animal life, fertile soil, natural shelter

Practice (Three's a Crowd)

1. fossil fuel
2. cultural features
3. terrain
4. involuntary
5. abundance
6. mass migration
7. subduction zone
8. population
9. Indigenous people
10. subsistence farming

Practice (Cause and Effect)

1. C
2. E
3. F
4. G
5. D
6. A
7. B

Practice (Summarizing)

Answers will vary. Possible answers:

Lesson 55: Maps tell the story of a place through its landforms, waterways, and position in the world.

Lesson 56: When humans settle, they consider landforms and available resources to determine where to live.

Lesson 57: People adapt to their environment when they settle in a location.

Lesson 58: Indigenous peoples are the first people to settle in an area, and the ways Indigenous South Americans used the land and its resources continues to influence the way humans settle and live in the environment today.

Lesson 59: The environment changes over time due to physical processes and human changes.

Lesson 60: Because South America has regions that are very different, the resources available in each reason are also different.

Lesson 61: Some of South America's most valuable natural resources are timber, iron ore, copper, silver, petroleum, coffee, bananas, and wool.

Lesson 62: Sometimes people migrate voluntarily or involuntarily.

Lesson 63: Because many people from all over the world have settled in South America, lots of different cultures have helped to create new cultural expressions that blend features together. Culture is a part of everyday life.

Lesson 64: South America influences the world with their culture by attracting people to come to South America to visit, study, and work.

Quick Review

Refer to the statement your student circled in the Show What You Know section to self-assess their knowledge of the chapter concepts. Then to assist in determining if your student is ready to take the assessment, consider:

- Having your student review what they are struggling with from the lessons in this chapter.

Chapter Assessment

Read each sentence. Circle True or False

1. True or False   Figs are South America's biggest agricultural export.

2. True or False   The Patagonian Desert is arid and cold.

3. True or False   In downtown Lima, Peru, there are ruins from a very old civilization called Huaca Pucllana that were once used for irrigation and ceremonies.

4. True or False   Shakira and Juanes are South Americans famous for their athletic performance.

5. True or False   The governments of South America have tried to create an intergovernmental organization, but they are having trouble sticking to an agreement.

Match each vocabulary term to its definition.

6. _____ human settlement

7. _____ mass migration

8. _____ climatic process

9. _____ geologic process

10. _____ ore deposits

11. _____ terrain

12. _____ deforested

13. _____ subsistence farming

14. _____ cultural features

15. _____ cultural diplomacy

A. interactions in nature that relate to the climate

B. large quantities of a particular mineral

C. the act of sharing culture with the world

D. many people moved around the same time for similar reasons

E. physical features

F. family farmers that harvest just enough crops to feed themselves

G. a place where people live

H. unique traditions or aspects of a culture such as language, religion, and dress

I. the process involving how Earth or its surface is changed

J. forest or trees have been removed from an area

Answer the following question in complete sentences.

16. Is South America culturally diverse?

....

....

....

Chapter Assessment Answer Key

1. False
2. True
3. True
4. False
5. True
6. G
7. D
8. A
9. I
10. B
11. E
12. J
13. F
14. H
15. C
16. Answers may vary. Possible answer: South America is very diverse culturally because there are many different groups of people that have influenced the development of culture across the continent. Different people live in each country and region in South America. They also have different languages, styles of dress, and customs. Many of these things have been influenced by the mixing of cultures that has happened over time between Indigenous peoples, European colonizers, immigrants, and enslaved Africans. This has created very rich traditions in South American cultures.

Alternative Assessment

Project: Magazine Article

A magazine article is an independent piece of narrative writing within a larger work. Magazine articles are sometimes short enough to fit on one page, but give enough information for the reader to clearly understand the topic.

Project Requirements:

For this project, design a magazine article that addresses an issue discussed in the chapter. If needed, research some relevant and recent issues that can be written about from your perspective.

Include the following elements in the magazine article:

- Title or headline
- Date
- Sources
- A fluid and intriguing progression of the subject and writing

Discover! SOCIAL STUDIES • GRADE 5 • CHAPTER 6 ASSESSMENT

173

Alternative Assessment Rubric

Use the following rubric to grade your student's assessment.

	4	3	2	1	Points
Research	The magazine article provides detailed and factual information and the topic is thoroughly researched.	The magazine article has some detailed and factual information and the topic is thoroughly researched.	The magazine article has very little detailed and factual information and the topic is not thoroughly researched.	The magazine article does not provide detailed and factual information and the topic is not thoroughly researched.	
Perspective and Interest	The magazine article provides a unique perspective on the topic and the writing is well developed.	The magazine article provides a unique perspective on the topic but the writing could be more well developed.	The magazine article provides very little unique perspective on the topic and the writing is not well developed.	The magazine article does not provide a unique perspective on the topic and the writing is not well developed.	
Required Elements	The magazine article makes clear and repetitive connections to the unit and includes all the required elements.	The magazine article is related to the unit but does not include all the required elements.	The magazine article makes one or two references to the unit but does not include all the required elements.	The magazine article is unrelated to the unit and does not include all the required elements.	
Grammar and Mechanics	The magazine article has no grammar mistakes and uses advanced vocabulary.	The magazine article contains a few grammar mistakes and uses age-appropriate vocabulary.	The magazine article contains several grammar mistakes and age-appropriate vocabulary.	The magazine article contains a distracting number of grammar issues and uses oversimplified vocabulary.	

Total Points _____/16

Average _____

Lesson Objectives

By the end of this lesson, your student will be able to:

- examine different maps of Oceania
- determine what story each map tells
- identify major cities in Oceania and locate them on a map
- compare and contrast the location of major cities in Oceania to the location of cities in your community with respect to nearby geographic features

Supporting Your Student

Read (Oceania)

As your student reads about Oceania, locate Australia, New Zealand, and the Pacific Island regions on the map. As your student learns about Oceania, think about or refer back to the map displaying all of the continents. Talk about how this region differs from other continents. For example, it is made up of islands, the land area is smaller, and the ocean surrounds all the land area.

Engage your student in a discussion that allows them to explore the Pacific Islands in Oceania. Ask, "Have you ever been to an island or a town near an ocean or lake before? What do you remember about it?" (People lived in houses near the water. There were lots of things to do that involved the water such as swimming, boating, surfing, etc. Everyone was attracted to the water area.) Provide examples from experiences you may have had. Ask,"Have you ever heard of any of the islands located in Oceania?" (Fiji, Bora Bora)

Read (The Stories in Maps of Oceania)

As your student explores the map of Australia, ask them to begin by identifying what type of map this is. They should be able to identify that it is a topographic map. Create a color chart with your student to show the color and the corresponding landform or type. For example, color a blue square and then next to it write "bodies of water." This way your student can reference this chart when writing about the story of this map.

Read (Identifying Locations in Oceania)

Read the section and refer to the political map. Play a partner game with your student. The first partner asks, "Can you put a star next to the region of Queensland (or any other region)?" The second partner asks a different question. "Can you put a triangle next to the city of Darwin?" Be sure to have your student identify whether the location is a region or city. The question should be arranged in this order: "Can you put a _____ next to the region or city of _____?"

Read (Major Cities in Oceania)

Using the chart, read about the cities in Oceania. Use the previous maps to locate them.

Write (How is your hometown similar or different to Oceania? What features are significant to your hometown?)

In this activity, your student is comparing their hometown or state to a city in Oceania. If your student struggles to see a personal connection to one of the cities in Oceania, then guide them to think about major cities they have learned about in the other chapters they have completed. Engage them in a discussion of how one of those cities is like one in Oceania. For example, "Baltimore, Maryland, has a harbor and Sydney has a harbor. My state has a governor just like Sydney has a governor."

Practice

Mark the locations on the map. Follow the directions to have your student engage with the map.

Learning Styles

Auditory learners may enjoy telling a story about their hometown or state.

Visual learners may enjoy researching additional types of maps to learn more stories about Oceania.

Kinesthetic learners may enjoy building a large-scale map of Oceania, and then walking the outlines of the countries on the continent or jumping from one island to another.

Extension Activities

Another Kind of Map

To help build more understanding of the continent of Oceania, have your student explore a population map. As they look at the population map, have them create a chart of each country and list the population of each one. When they are complete, ask them to provide a hypothesis as to why one region might be more populated than another.

Great Barrier Reef

Your student briefly learned about the Great Barrier Reef. If your student is interested in learning more, have them research how the Great Barrier Reef has changed over time. Then have your student create a timeline showing the evolution of the Great Barrier Reef.

Answer Key

Write *(Looking at the topographic map of Australia, what story do you think could be told about the water? What story could you tell about the green areas of the map?)*

1. Answers will vary. Possible answers: This is a topographic map that shows the elevations of the land. The green areas show forested areas or grasslands, and the blue shows the rivers, and surrounding ocean.

2. Answers will vary. Possible answers: There are only a few areas of green on the map. Therefore, the country has more land area that is dry and forms a desert. People most likely live around the edge or coasts of Australia because it is more favorable than the dry, arid deserts in the middle of the country.

Write *(How is your hometown similar or different to Oceania? What features are significant to your hometown?)*

Answers will vary. Possible answer: My hometown is not surrounded by water. We only speak one main language there. Sydney is surrounded by water, and over 250 languages are spoken there.

Practice

NEW ZEALAND MAP

Show What You Know

1. A

2. B

3.

4. Answers will vary. Possible answer: Sydney being similar in population size, or surrounded by water.

Lesson Objectives

By the end of this lesson, your student will be able to:

- analyze geographic factors that influence where people live in Oceania
- identify the significance of key geographic features of Oceania
- compare and contrast patterns of human settlements of different regions in Oceania and analyze how the environment influenced these settlements

Supporting Your Student

Write *(According to the population density map, where do most people live? Which geographical feature is present in the area with most of the people?)*

Talk with your student about the advantages and disadvantages of living on the coast or in the desert. Share your thoughts about where you would rather live and why. Discuss with your student how to read a population density map. Take a look at the map key together and discuss what the different colors indicate on the map. Talk about where the different colored dots appear on the map. Remind your student that the size of the circles means a larger population of people. Smaller circles indicate fewer people but may appear more frequently on the map.

Read *(Comparing the Settlement Regions of Oceania)*

As your student is comparing the regions of Oceania, they should focus on the characteristics of human settlements. As they are looking at this category, engage them in discussing how one region compares to another. As they look at the provided map of each region, engage them in a discussion of why one area might have had access to better settlements than another.

Practice

Discuss with your student what people living in the picture may like to do or work they may enjoy on a typical day. Refer to the regions on page five to gain ideas about how the people in this region live their daily lives. Think about key parts of the day such as morning or meal times and what the people may do during these times. Discuss what kinds of activities they might do in their free time.

Learning Styles

Auditory learners may enjoy listening to the sounds of the animals that live in the rainforests of Papua New Guinea.

Visual learners may enjoy watching informational videos or excerpts of videos about the Great Barrier Reef.

Kinesthetic learners may enjoy using chalk to draw outlines of the countries in Oceania and identifying the regions.

Extension Activities

Shipwrecks of Oceania

One of the most common tourist adventures in Oceania is to go deep-sea diving to see the shipwrecks. Micronesia is one of the most famous regions to see shipwrecks. Have your student research to learn more about these shipwrecks and select one to create a drawing of. Have them create an undersea drawing of the shipwreck, showing the approximate location of it and the approximate sinking date.

Animals of the Great Victoria Desert

Oceania is home to many unique animals. Have your student research some of the popular animals that have learned to survive in the Great Victoria Desert. Have them create a digital slideshow that shows the animals and what adaptations they have made in order to survive in the desert.

Answer Key

Write *(According to the population density map, where do most people live? Which geographical feature is present in the area with most of the people?)*

Answers will vary. Possible answers: The map shows that most of the people live near the coast. The people live there because they are able to live in a comfortable climate and have access to water, food, and fertile land.

Practice

Answers will vary. Possible answers: The people who live here most likely enjoy water activities like swimming or canoeing. They probably eat fish for many meals and catch the fish themselves. They may work to catch fish for someone else to sell to others further inland. They probably cook their own breakfast and then go to work or school. They may go to a small town to purchase items or see friends during the day. At night they may enjoy the quiet beach.

Show What You Know

1. A

2. A, B, C

3. A

4. Answers will vary. Possible answer: The Great Barrier Reef is the largest coral reef system in the world, with more than 2,900 islands. It also has a large biodiversity.

Lesson Objectives

By the end of this lesson, your student will be able to:

- investigate the physical geography of Oceania
- analyze the effects of the influence of people's relationship to natural resources on the development of various Oceanian civilizations

Supporting Your Student

Explore

There are many previous lessons covering landforms in the fifth grade curriculum and in previous grades. This lesson is the first to concentrate on islands and how they form. Your student may have trouble thinking about landforms underwater. One way to help them imagine this is to look up recent pictures of Mars. Challenge your student to name the landforms they see, then imagine Mars as a planet with oceans and lakes. Where would the landforms go?

Read (Continental Islands)

As your student is reading about the physical geography of Oceania, it might be best to have a map available to them. They can use the map to help them identify the regions and how each of those regions were formed. This map may help:

Read (Fire and Water)

Volcanoes are a perennial favorite with students of all ages. Help your student do some online research about volcanoes to find interesting and useful information.

Read (Ridges and Reefs)

There are many ways to learn more about reefs both online and by watching documentaries. Help your student understand how reefs are essential to many species of fish as a breeding ground, a home, and a place to find food. Some documentaries may explain the role that reefs play in protecting against coastal erosion caused by storms.

Learning Styles

Auditory learners may enjoy listening to the languages of the Indigenous people. There is also a long tradition of music made by drumming in Oceania.

Visual learners may enjoy looking at pictures and videos of the Indigenous people, but preview the pictures and videos before showing your student.

Kinesthetic learners might enjoy creating a yard-sized map of Oceania. Everyday objects of different sizes could represent Australia, New Guinea, New Zealand, Hawaii, etc. Encourage your student to think about relative distances when placing their islands.

Extension Activities

Surfing

Surfing was once the sport of Hawaiian royalty. Now, it is a world-wide activity and competitive sport. Your student could research both the origins of surfing and where to find the big waves today.

Plan a Visit

Oceania is a tourist destination, but it really takes planning to visit such a vast continent. Have your student plan a trip to a destination in Oceania that includes travel time, a visit to a geographic marvel (i.e., volcano, reef, rainforest, desert), and a place of scientific investigation (i.e., a habitat, nature preserve, observatory). Help your student weave the lessons they've learned from all their studies this year into a single activity.

Answer Key

Explore
Your student should choose either Australia or Oceania. Encourage them to explain their logic.

Show What You Know
1. continental
2. A
3. C
4. reef system
5. Answers will vary but should include fishing at the least. More complete answers will include that they found food and that they brought new foods with them like taro and pigs.

Lesson Objectives

By the end of this lesson, your student will be able to:

- extend understanding that people make and respond to changes to their environment in various ways
- analyze the effects that the introduction of agriculture had on newly settled regions
- examine other ways that people in Oceania made changes to their environment
- illustrate examples of how they responded to changes in the environment

Supporting Your Student

Read (Papua New Guinea)

Help your student understand that people are finding solutions in nature to build safer environments. Your student may enjoy researching online how mangroves fight erosion.

Read (Effects of Agriculture)

As your student reads about the changes in Oceania, define for them what a solar farm is and how using solar power is helpful in generating power. Solar farms are large collections of photovoltaic (PV) solar panels that absorb energy from the sun, turn it into electricity, and then send that electricity to the power grid for public use. Solar power is often referred to as "clean energy" since you are using just the sun to create electricity, instead of traditional materials like coal. Ask your student to think about any solar farms, or panels, that they may have seen where they live. Engage them in a discussion of why Australia might be a very good place to use solar power.

Write (Using the information above, complete this chart.)

As your student's reading ability progresses, the texts they encounter imply ideas more and more often to encourage the reader's imagination and critical-thinking skills. This task is a deliberate skill-building task.

Practice

Engage your student in a discussion of what happened when the Māori people cleared the forests in their area. Have them refer back to the text, and highlight or underline this information so they can complete the chart.

Learning Styles

Auditory learners may enjoy listening to stories about Suva, Fiji, and how it evolved over time into a big city.

Visual learners may enjoy seeing photos or videos of the solar and wind farms to see how they are established in the Oceanic countries.

Kinesthetic learners may enjoy planting a plant in regular soil and one in salty soil and recording the differences they notice in the way the plant grows.

Extension Activities

Create a Windmill

Have your student create a windmill of their own. They may do this by using an online search engine to search for directions, or you may just give them materials (a toilet paper tube, wooden skewers, cardstock paper, glue, decor items) and tell them to create a windmill. Once their windmill has been created, ask them how a windmill might be used to generate electricity for people.

Bird Species

As your student learned in this lesson, many bird species went extinct as the Māori people cleared land for agriculture. Have your student research the most common types of bird species in New Zealand and where they are on the list of potentially endangered animals. Have your student create a chart that shows what they have learned.

Answer Key

In the Real World

Answers will vary. The issue of dams and reservoirs affect communities everywhere. Your student may focus on who owned the land set aside for the reservoir, the destruction of habitat, or the destruction of cultural heritage like cemeteries or Indigenous sites. They may bring up ideas covered in other lessons. Your student may also focus on the positives like drinking water and water sports. If their response is one-sided, you may choose to ask them to consider the other side too.

Write (Describe how the people of Papua New Guinea responded to the destruction of agricultural land and fisheries due to the OK Tedi Mine.)

Answers will vary. Possible answer: The people decided to speak up and reach an agreement with the Ok Tedi Mine so that they would clean up the leftover sediments in the water and reestablish the clean water area.

Write (The text lists several positive and negative effects of agriculture. Use the information above to complete the chart.)

Answers will vary. Possible answers:

New Zealand

Positive Effects: Māori farmers fed their people successfully

Negative Effects: loss of trees changes the ecosystem, extinct species left holes in the ecosystem and food-chain, tree cover was cut in half, 40 species of birds went extinct

Australia

Positive Effects: modern agriculture feeds a lot of hungry people

Negative Effects: the practice may add to the droughts, the practice may not be sustainable, caused erosion, increased salinity leads to soil infertility, drought resistant native plants were removed from the ecosystem

Practice

Answers will vary depending on your region. Solar options are popular in Florida and the desert southwest of the United States while wind options are popular on plains and coasts. Water-based options are popular wherever rivers flow through valleys. If your student focuses on land, air, or water quality/usage, the answer will vary according to the community's needs and response.

Show What You Know

1. A
2. C
3. sun or sunlight
4. wind
5. change
6. Answers will vary. Possible answers: The mine destroyed local fisheries and agricultural land because of the toxins going into the river.

Lesson Objectives

By the end of this lesson, your student will be able to:

- identify the physical processes that contribute to the availability and abundance of a natural resource
- compare and contrast the availability and distribution of natural resources in Oceania across regions

Supporting Your Student

Explore

Your student could benefit from understanding that the plant life of Oceania is both uniformly tropical throughout the islands and interestingly unique. A species of flower or plant may exist on only one island. Birds, storms, tides, currents, and winds have played a major part in spreading life around the islands. Human migration has also played a part, especially in spreading animals such as pigs and chickens. Understanding that information could help your student connect with the information in this section and its significance.

Read (Physical Processes)

One way to help your student is to search online for some kid-friendly videos about the coastal processes of erosion, coastal landforms, and tectonic activity. Watching these physical processes in action could help your student connect with the effects they have on the environment more easily and effectively.

Read (Natural Resources)

The cattle and sheep in the region were brought by Asian and European settlers. This has impacted the traditional natural inhabitants of Australia and New Zealand, including the extinction of the Tasmanian tiger (also called the Tasmanian wolf or thylacine). Rabbits, deer, mice, and rats brought by Europeans have caused environmental problems due to the low number of natural predators. This is a connection to food chain studies your student has covered in science.

Learning Styles

Auditory learners may enjoy listening to the stories of how the sheep came to New Zealand.

Visual learners may enjoy watching videos of the different physical processes learned in this lesson.

Kinesthetic learners may enjoy creating a model that demonstrates erosion activity with a small baking pan, sand, small rocks, and water. Place sand at one end of the pan and create a landmass that slopes toward the opposite end, leaving some empty space to represent the sea. Use your finger to create a river from the top of the sand to the bottom, and line both sides of it with the rocks. Then gently pour the water in at the top of the "river" and watch as it erodes some of the sand and rocks on its way toward the sea.

Extension Activities

Fiji Mini Book

Fiji is one of the islands formed by volcanic activity. Have your student research how Fiji was formed and what natural resources can be found there as a result of its physical process. Have your student create a mini book that describes their research.

Tsunami News Report

Giant waves known as tsunamis are a common physical process in the Pacific Islands. Have your student research a recent tsunami that has occurred in the Pacific Islands. Then have them act as a news reporter or journalist that is reporting on the story of the tsunami. They may choose to provide a live news report to you or write a news article.

Answer Key

Explore

Answers will vary. Possible answers: Birds can carry seeds to an island, and that plant can begin to grow there. Those plants could be edible and provide food for humans, which could cause them to settle there and develop a civilization.

Practice

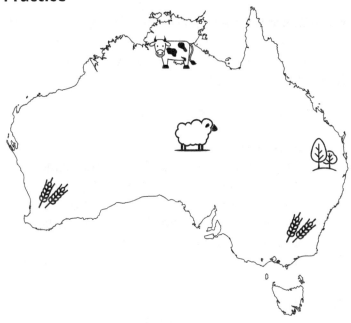

Show What You Know

1. B
2. A, C
3. A
4. Answers will vary. Possible answer: The larger islands of Australasia have more land to use for agriculture, mining, and fishing. The smaller islands have just enough land to grow enough food to support their populations.

Lesson Objectives

By the end of this lesson, your student will be able to:

- identify key natural resources found in Oceania
- describe how the use, distribution, and importance of natural resources can affect different groups
- identify the impact of trade on the availability of natural resources

Supporting Your Student

Write *(What are the key natural resources in the Pacific Islands?)*

As your student reflects on the key natural resources in the Pacific Islands, instruct them to return to the natural resources of the Pacific Islands listed on page 3. If they are unsure of the natural resources, refer them back to the definition of a natural resource: things found in nature that can be used by people. Talk with your student about some of the natural resources listed in the chart and ask guiding questions about how the resources could be used.

Read *(Trade)*

As your student reads about trade in Oceania, have them refer to a map to understand why China plays such an important role with trade in the countries in Oceania. Explain that China is in close proximity to Oceania, so therefore it is a more ideal location for trade. Discuss with them the impacts of how trade can benefit each country. Explain that as a resource increases, competition increases and lowers world prices.

Practice

As your student reflects on how natural resources are distributed across Oceania, they should refer back to the text in the Read "Trade" section. Have your student try to paraphrase what they learned in their own words.

Learning Styles

Auditory learners may enjoy listening to the people of Papua New Guinea singing cultural songs and coordinating dances. Search for videos or auditory clips to enjoy.

Visual learners may enjoy watching videos of New Zealand sheep grazing in the farmland as well as seeing them sheared for their wool.

Kinesthetic learners may enjoy drawing a picture of each resource and creating a motion to go with each. For example, the motion for wood would be the act of chopping down a tree.

Extension Activities

Vanilla in Tonga

One of the most exported goods from the island of Tonga in Oceania is the vanilla bean. Have your student research to learn more about the process of harvesting vanilla in Tonga. If you have vanilla in your house, smell the vanilla and enjoy the scent. Talk about other things around your house that may be flavored with vanilla (i.e., pudding, lotion, oils).

Wood Chips

As your student learned, Australia produces wood chips. Your student may be familiar with the use of wood chips on local playgrounds. Have them research other uses for wood chips. To present the information to you, have them create a collage of pictures that shows the other uses for wood chips.

Answer Key

Write *(What are the key natural resources in the Pacific Islands?)*

Answers will vary. Possible answer: The key natural resources are bananas, fishing, kava, sugarcane, and vanilla.

Practice

Answers will vary. Possible answers:

Wood: There is 17 percent forest land in Australia. Other countries could provide resources not found in their country in return for wood products.

Fish: Fish is abundant in the Pacific Islands. Countries in the Pacific Islands might deplete their resources because of trade with China.

Show What You Know

1. A

2. B

3. infrastructure

4. Answers will vary. Possible answer: Trade may increase the demand or need for a product such as wood and therefore quickly deplete that natural resource. In addition, there may not be any wood left to use locally.

5. Answers will vary. Possible answer: New Zealand does not have enough wood for future trade opportunities. The demand for bananas may not be high enough to be able to sell to other countries. New Zealand would lose opportunities for trade.

Lesson Objectives

By the end of this lesson, your student will be able to:

• extend understanding that human migration is influenced by both known and unknown factors

• identify the factors that led to the immigration of people from one region in Oceania

• examine the factors that contributed to the Polynesian Migrations and analyze the evidence supporting each factor

• examine the contributions of migrants from one region in Oceania to another

Supporting Your Student

Read (Factors of Migration)

Start by reading the introductory paragraph. Before reading this page, have your student stand. As they read aloud the push factors, have them push their hand against a nearby table or wall. For the pull factors, lean back and pretend to pull while reading this section. Interjecting movement into learning can help your brain remember new information.

Write (Choose three keywords and write a sentence about the factors that influence moving in Oceania.)

This page describes the factors for moving to regions of Oceania and from regions of Oceania. While rereading this page, have your student underline or highlight keywords. Tell your student these would be the most important words or words that would give them the "key" to unlock the ideas in this page.

Read (Polynesian Migration)

The large map of the Pacific Islands is pictured in this section. Your student is directed to circle the area of Polynesia on the map. If your student needs assistance with this, refer them to Lesson 67. Remind them that Oceania is divided into four settlement regions. They can refer to the map located in this lesson to circle the Polynesia region.

Learning Styles

Auditory learners may enjoy making a rap about what they have learned. Your student may want to record themselves to share with someone. Alternatively, your student could perform the rap for family or friends.

Visual learners may enjoy researching maps of migration in the Oceania region. Maps can be found online, but may not always represent the same migration patterns. Researchers are still not sure of the exact path the migrants took.

Kinesthetic learners may enjoy drawing representations of the countries with simple circles on a large piece of paper or outside with chalk. Then have them use large markers to draw lines between the countries. Use an online tool to research migration maps for reference.

Extension Activities

Navigating With Stars

Early settlers in Oceania sailed across the ocean using the stars as one of their tools to guide them. Have your student take a look online and research which stars can be used to navigate and draw a small picture with labels. If they are feeling adventurous, have them take a look outside at night to see if you can locate any of these stars.

Polynesian Canoes

Have your student title a piece of construction paper *Polynesian Canoes*. Then have them fold the piece of paper into thirds and label the columns *Pictures*, *Materials*, and *Supplies*. Have them research "Polynesian Voyaging Canoes" and look for facts, words, or phrases to include in each column.

Answer Key

Write *(Choose three keywords and write a sentence about the factors that influence moving in Oceania.)*
Answers will vary. Possible answers:

1. Jobs; People move to New Zealand for new job opportunities.
2. Climate changes; People move from Papua New Guinea because they may have experienced extreme climate changes.
3. Scenery; People move to Australia because of the beautiful scenery.

Write *(How were the Polynesians able to sail to islands far away?)*
Answers will vary. Possible answers: Polynesians were able to migrate because of the changing high winds and the large voyaging canoes they built.

Write *(Make a list of three ways migrants in Oceania contributed to society.)*
Answers will vary. Possible answers:

1. farming techniques such as sweet potatoes and other vegetables
2. the creation of weapons carved out of wood
3. knowledge of the ocean and navigation through the use of the stars

Show What You Know

1. B
2. A
3. migration
4. voyaging canoes, wind factors
5. Answers will vary. Possible answers: Someone may move to Australia in search of beautiful scenery or a seasonal job opportunity.

Lesson Objectives

By the end of this lesson, your student will be able to:

• identify cultural features of Oceania
• describe how cultural features in a region of Oceania influence factors of daily life such as economy, government, or transportation

Supporting Your Student

Read (Cultural Features)

As you read about the cultural features of Oceania, think about how your student may make a personal connection with each category of cultural features. For example, ask, "Have you seen an artifact before? Where was it? Do you remember a unique architectural building? What works of art are you familiar with? What story did each tell?" Give your student some personal examples as well.

Read (Influences of Cultural Features)

For this section, have your student fold a piece of paper in half. Before reading each paragraph, have your student read the heading and predict the information in the paragraph that will follow. For example, the picture of a house may describe how people are spread out from one another, making the population small. Then read the paragraph. Continue this activity for each influence. For the sections on government and transportation, it may be helpful to look up these places online with your student. For example, your student may look up the Parliament House in Canberra to learn more about what takes place there. Additionally, your student may look up different types of public transportation that is popular in Australia besides buses.

Learning Styles

Auditory learners may enjoy listening to the word *hello* in the many languages of Oceania. (Other words may be used as well.) Use the internet to search for the most popular languages of Oceania and listen to *hello* in those languages.

Visual learners may enjoy exploring more about the different types of dress of the countries of Oceania. Use the internet to search for "traditional dress in (insert country name)." Ask them to identify two of their favorite outfits.

Kinesthetic learners may enjoy creating their own rock art. You may find rocks from your backyard or local park and have your student paint rock art like the Aboriginal people. Try to think of symbols that would represent your country, region, or family. Alternatively, use a paper plate or colored piece of construction paper as your surface.

Extension Activities

Traditions of Oceania

Have your student create a travel brochure for the Oceania region using cultural features. Have them fold a piece of paper into thirds and choose a cultural feature for each section to "advertise" the region to others who may want to come to visit.

Bark Paintings

Aboriginal artists painted on the bark of eucalyptus trees because they shed larger pieces of the bark each year. Using a brown paper bag, have your student cut a section that can be painted or colored. Have them decorate the paper like a piece of bark art. For ideas, look online using the keywords "Aboriginal eucalyptus bark art."

Answer Key

Write *(Choose one of the cultural features above and describe its significance.)*
Answers will vary. Possible answer: The Beehive building in New Zealand is significant because meetings are held there for the government officials.

Write *(How do the arts influence the economy in Papua New Guinea?)*
Answers will vary. Possible answer: Artists sell their work at festivals and tourist areas in order to make money. They make connections with each other in order to plan other events and sell their works.

Write *(Choose either transportation or government and describe how it has influenced the people of Australia and New Zealand.)*
Answers will vary. Possible answer: The bus system in New Zealand allows people to go from the North Island to the South Island. The government of Australia was brought together by the process of building the Parliament building. It is a sign of their country's strength.

Show What You Know

1. B
2. A
3. rocks, eucalyptus tree bark
4. tradition
5. buses
6. festivals and tourist areas
7. Answers will vary. Possible answer: Aboriginal rock art is significant because it was used for important rituals and ceremonies. It left a lasting mark on their culture.

Lesson Objectives

By the end of this lesson, your student will be able to:

- investigate the cultural geography of Oceania
- explore broader influences of Oceanian culture on individuals and civilizations around the world
- discover the lasting impact of Oceanian culture on everyday aspects of life

Supporting Your Student

Read *(Cultural Geography of Oceania)*

As your student explores the arts in Oceania, they may need a reference to what some of the art items are. Research online to show them examples of Australian and New Zealand wood carvings. Engage them in a discussion on how storytelling is an important aspect of culture. It is important because that is often how information is passed on from one group of people to another.

Read *(Influences Around the World)*

As your student reads about how Oceania has influenced the world, engage them in a discussion of what it means to influence something. To influence is to effect change indirectly but in an important way. As they are exploring how the subjects listed have influenced the world, discuss how the creators might not have intended for these to be world-changing. For example, the Sydney Opera House was built to enlighten the community of Sydney. Even though it had accomplished that goal, it has also become a landmark known around the world.

Practice

As your student explores the impact of wool, the black box recorder, and the Sydney Opera House, it would be best to engage them in a discussion of what it means to have a lasting impact on something. When a lasting impact exists, the item or subject continues to exist or has an effect for a very long time. Your student may make a personal reference here to describe something that has had a lasting impact in their life.

Learning Styles

Auditory learners may enjoy listening to some of the storytelling from the Aboriginals. Use the internet to look for original storytelling works. Have your student choose a favorite to share with a friend or family member.

Visual learners may enjoy researching and looking at the wood carvings of the Australian and New Zealand people. Have your student print out several interesting pictures and label them to share with others.

Kinesthetic learners may enjoy trying to recreate the building of the Sydney Opera House. The designer said he was inspired by the peeling of an orange. You may have your student try to use orange peels to create the building or some other type of building block.

Extension Activities

Discover Moai Sculptures

Have your student research the moai stone sculptures made by the Rapa Nui people of Easter Island. Have them search for images of the sculptures and look for answers to these questions: "Why is it called 'Easter Island'?" and "What eventually happened to the people who made these sculptures?" These massive stone sculptures have made a long-lasting impression on people around the world for centuries.

Haka Dance

The country of New Zealand is famous for its exceptional rugby teams. They even have a special dance to get the fans excited for the game called the haka. It is based on a war dance that prepared the Māori people for battle. What do you think *haka* means? Have your student search online for a video of the special dance to see how this tradition brings the people of New Zealand together and connects them to their past.

Answer Key

Write *(How have people through the generations shaped the arts, foods, or tourism in Oceania?)*

Answers will vary. Possible answer: People have engaged in storytelling and wood carvings. Wood carvings are still popular today in Oceania. People told stories to their children and then again to their children's children.

Practice

Answers will vary. Possible answers:

1. wool: People prefer New Zealand wool because of its cleanliness.
2. black box recorder: The black box is used in most airplanes around the world.
3. Sydney Opera House: People come from around the world to visit the opera house and watch performances.

Show What You Know

1. B
2. cochlear
3. Answers will vary. Possible answer: Sydney Opera House, *Lord of the Rings* movies, cochlear implants or bionic ear, ultrasound scanner, black box
4. Answers will vary. Possible answer: The opera house attracts millions of visitors worldwide just to see the building, and a million more to view performances there.

Lesson Objectives

By the end of this lesson, your student will review the following big ideas from Chapter 7.

- Maps can tell many different stories. (Lesson 66)
- Geographic features influence where people live. (Lesson 67)
- Physical geography influences people's relationships with natural resources. (Lesson 68)
- People make changes to their environment. (Lesson 69)
- Physical processes can lead to the availability of resources. (Lesson 70)
- There are major natural resources in Oceania. (Lesson 71)
- The people of Oceania migrated from one area to another. (Lesson 72)
- Cultural features influence populations. (Lesson 73)
- Cultural geography exists in Oceania and makes a lasting impact worldwide. (Lesson 74)

Supporting Your Student

Create

For this writing activity, your student has to think of themselves in "someone else's shoes." Your student may be able to write about a day in the life of a student on an Oceanic island or country. As they write, try to pull out different ideas that connect to the ideas learned in the chapter. Ask, "What were they able to eat?" "What landforms could they see or experience?" "Did they create some type of art to represent themselves?" "Did they live close to a lot of people?"

Read (Maps and Geography of Oceania)

As your student looks at the maps, have them refer back to Lesson 66. Be sure they label what type of map each picture shows, and include a few details about the story the map tells. If they are struggling, prompt them with a few questions like, "What stands out to you on the map?" "How are the maps different from each other?" "What color is represented the most? Why?"

Practice (Oceania Board Game)

This should be an engaging and fun activity for your student. Encourage them to be creative with the game and include geographical features of Oceania on the board. Have your student look back through the lessons to come up with questions for the game. Noting the answers somewhere is also helpful. Encourage your student to "be the teacher" and come up with challenging questions for the game. When it is finished, have your student play with a family member or friend.

Learning Styles

Auditory learners may enjoy recording facts from each lesson and then replay those facts back. Your student can read the summary items directly from the text or write their own.

Visual learners may enjoy reviewing all of the different types of maps that were used in this chapter. In addition, your student may want to research additional maps online to make connections with the information they have learned.

Kinesthetic learners may enjoy making a clay representation of the countries in Oceania. If possible, label a few other geographical features or meaningful locations once the clay representation has dried.

Extension Activities

Protecting the Coral Reef

Global warming and climate change have affected the reef. They have caused slow damage to the reef. Have your student research ways to prevent continual damage to the reef. Have them organize their ideas into a letter to the editor for an Australian newspaper convincing people to take action to save the reef.

Kangaroos

Kangaroos are often associated with the country of Australia. Besides the fact that kangaroos live in the country, how else are they significant? Have your student make a small poster with facts about kangaroos but also include why they are a symbol for the people of Australia.

Answer Key

Write *(Look at these maps of Australia. Write whether each map is a topographic map or a geopolitical map. Then write two to three sentences about what stories these maps tell.)*

Answers will vary. Possible answers: The map on the right is a geopolitical map of Australia. It shows political borders for counties and states. It includes locations for cities and capitals. Most of the cities are located in the coastal areas. The map on the left is a topographic map that shows the elevation of the land. The green areas are forests or grasslands. The blue shows rivers and surrounding ocean. There are only a few areas of green on the map, therefore Australia has a larger amount of brown areas that indicate a desert.

Practice *(Three's a Crowd)*

1. solar farms; Erosion and land clearing are effects of agriculture on the land.
2. Auckland; Melbourne and Sydney are cities in Australia.
3. deserts; Oceania islands formed from volcanoes and limestone.
4. New Zealand; Melanesia and Micronesia are regions in Oceania.
5. birds; Forest products and fishing are natural resources.
6. oranges; Bananas and eucalyptus grow in Oceania.
7. deserts; Voyaging canoes and high winds enabled the discovery of Polynesain islands.
8. computers; Cochlear implants and black boxes were created in Oceania.
9. desert; Volcanic and coral are types of islands.

Practice *(Change in Oceania)*

Answers will vary. Possible answer:

Positive Effects: Maori farmers feed their people successfully

Negative Effects: loss of trees changes the ecosystem, extinct species left holes in the ecosystem or food chain, increased salinity leads to soil infertility

Practice *(Oceania Board Game)*

Answers will vary based on what type of game your student creates.

Quick Review

Refer to the statement your student circled in the Show What You Know section to self-assess their knowledge of the chapter concepts. Then to assist in determining if your student is ready to take the assessment, consider:

- Having your student explain how the different types of maps tell different stories.
- Having your student name the natural resources found in Oceania.
- Having your student describe the physical and cultural geography of Oceania.

Chapter Assessment

Circle the correct answer.

1. True or False   Natural resources in Oceania include vanilla, coconut, rubber, and coffee.
2. True or False   A lagoon is a chain of islands.
3. True or False   Coconuts are a natural resource in Oceania.
4. True or False   The Polynesians used detailed maps to migrate to the islands of Oceania.
5. True or False   Australia has a large, arid desert.
6. True or False   Sydney is the capital of Australia.
7. True or False   Australia, New Zealand, and New Guinea are the major continental islands.
8. True or False   Degradation is breaking down something to make it more valuable.
9. True or False   Fish are a meal source in Oceania but are also exported to other countries.
10. True or False   Auckland, New Zealand, is the most populated city in that country.
11. True or False   Looking for a new job may be a reason to move to Australia.
12. The purpose of a _____ map is to highlight landforms.

   A. physical   **C.** climate

   B. political   **D.** resource

13. A map that is most similar to a physical map is a _____ map.

   A. political   **C.** resource

   B. climate   **D.** topographic

14. Oceanic migrants changed the ecosystems of their new home islands by introducing new _____.

   A. boats   **C.** erosion

   B. animals   **D.** mangroves

15. Most of the commercial fishing in Oceania is done by _____.

   A. locals   **C.** Micronesians

   B. Māori   **D.** foreigners

16. To counter erosion, some island nations are _____.

   A. planting mangroves   **C.** planting mandrakes

   B. planting mangoes   **D.** building dams

17. New Zealand is known for the quality of its _____ exports.

   A. mutton   **C.** cotton

   B. beef   **D.** wool

18. Oceania exports the most metals from _____.

   A. Micronesia   **C.** Melanesia

   B. Polynesia   **D.** Australasia

19. Human habitation of New Zealand has resulted in the extinction of several types of _____.

   A. sharks   **C.** mammals

   B. birds   **D.** marsupials

20. Tropical rainforests can be found in _____.

   A. Western Australia   **C.** Northern Australia

   B. Southern Australia   **D.** Tasmania

Use the Word Bank to fill in the blanks.

Word Bank:	ability	erosion	reef	water	windmills
	canoes	mountain	surface	weapons	

21. The _____ to use resources to support the economy is not equal in all countries of Oceania.

22. A coral _____ is an ocean feature that is made up of millions of coral skeletons.

23. Māori people made wooden defense _____ to protect their people.

24. Polynesians used voyaging _____ to cross the oceans in search of new islands.

25. New Zealand was in need of more modern electric power, so they built _____.

26. The Great Dividing Range is the largest _____ range in Australia, running along the entire east coast.

27. People settled near the coasts of Australia because they had access to _____ and fertile soil.

28. The process of breaking down rock by wind, water, or ice is called _____.

29. Tectonic activity pushes metals, minerals, and gems from earth's lower mantle closer to the _____ over time.

Answer the following question in complete sentences.

30. Explain why Australia is a good place to explore alternative energy solutions.

....

....

....

....

....

....

....

....

....

....

Discover! SOCIAL STUDIES • GRADE 5 • CHAPTER 7 ASSESSMENT

199

Chapter Assessment Answer Key

1. True
2. False
3. True
4. False
5. True
6. False
7. True
8. False
9. True
10. True
11. True
12. A
13. D
14. B
15. D
16. A
17. D
18. D
19. B
20. C
21. ability
22. coral reef
23. weapons
24. canoes
25. windmills
26. mountain
27. water
28. erosion
29. surface

30. Answers will vary. Possible answer: Australia's large desert and plains regions mean that solar energy is abundant.

Alternative Assessment

Project: Historical Fiction

Historical fiction is a piece of fictional literature that is based on or around a historical time period or event.

Project Requirements or Steps:

For this project, write a short piece of historical fiction based on an event or period in history from the chapter. You will exercise your research skills and work to convey a historical event or time period as realistically as possible.

Include the following elements:

1. Title related to the chapter
2. Reference to an important event or period in history on which the writing will be based
3. Plot progression or a clear storyline
4. Well-developed characters
5. Literary elements, such as figurative language
6. Connection to the chapter through setting, characters, plot, etc.

Alternative Assessment Rubric

Use the following rubric to grade your student's assessment.

	4	3	2	1	Points
Connection to the Chapter	The project is clearly connected to the chapter.	The project is connected to the chapter.	The project is somewhat connected to the chapter.	The project is not connected to the chapter.	
Creativity	The project is very creative and aesthetically appealing.	The project is creative and aesthetically appealing.	The project is somewhat creative and aesthetically appealing.	The project is not creative or aesthetically appealing.	
Information	The information or data is very accurate and easy to follow.	The information or data is accurate.	The information or data is somewhat accurate.	The information or data is not accurate..	
Grammar and Mechanics	There are no grammar or punctuation mistakes.	There are one or two grammar or punctuation mistakes.	There are several grammar or punctuation mistakes.	There are a distracting number of grammar or punctuation mistakes.	

Total Points _____/16

Average _____

202

Discover! SOCIAL STUDIES • GRADE 5 • CHAPTER 7 ASSESSMENT